Faith
from *the*
BackSide

More Books in the Back Side Series

J. Ellsworth Kalas

Faith *from* *the* BackSide

A Different Take On What It Means To Believe

Abingdon Press
Nashville

Faith from the Back Side

A Different Take on What It Means to Believe

This book is printed on acid-free paper.

Library of Congress Cataloging-in-Publication Data

Kalas, J. Ellsworth, 1923–
    Faith from the back side / J. Ellsworth Kalas.
        p.   cm.
    Includes bibiographical references (p.   ).
    ISBN 978-1-4267-4173-9 (pbk. : alk. paper)   1. Faith.   2. Christian life—Methodist authors.   I. Title.
    BV4637.K348   2011
    234'.23—dc23   2011032297

11 12 13 14 15 16 17 18 19 20—10 9 8 7 6 5 4 3 2 1

MANUFACTURED IN THE UNITED STATES OF AMERICA

Contents

CHAPTER ONE

Faith from the Back Side

Scripture Reading: Hebrews 10:39–11:1

Since you and I are human, faith comes to us naturally. In its raw form, it's as much a part of who we are as the air we breathe. I submit that a newborn cries out not only because she must have food, but also because she believes that if she asks, someone will provide the food. We're made that way. After all, we were fed for all those months in the womb without our even asking.

I watch (a bit nervously as I grow older) as a father throws a baby in the air and catches him while the baby squeals in delight. The baby has faith that he will be caught, else he would be terrified at being torn from his security and tossed into space. As time goes by the baby learns fear, which is the opposite of faith and at times an intelligent corrective. And it's good that he does, because without the caution that comes from fear, the infant life would quite easily be lost. Some of our fears are faith that has been educated and equipped for everyday living.

But we keep the basic structures of faith so that we can carry on our day-to-day business. We pour milk on our cereal believing it carries nourishment and not deadly germs. We trust that the cereal was packaged in a clean plant, and if we're health conscious we check the number of calories we're taking on and the ingredients in the cereal, believing that the message on the box is true. We have faith in the apparatus in our car as we back out of the garage. If we're traveling a familiar road to work or school or an appointment we have such faith in our memory that we all but let the automobile guide itself. If instead we're following a map or some electronic guide, we trust the road and street signs along the way. We live out our lives in a world of faith.

We ratchet the faith up several notches when we go to the doctor's office. The doctor gives support to our faith by a framed certificate on the wall of the examining room that testifies to years of medical training. When he or she says, "You have nothing to worry about," we answer, "You've made my day." And if instead the message is a prescription or a call for further examination, we usually extend our faith an extra step and do what the doctor tells us to do.

When we stop en route at a financial institution, we don't think twice about the fact that this particular place happens to be called a "bank and *trust* company," using a prime synonym for faith as part of its very name. Nor do we think as we take a credit card from our purse or wallet that the word *credit* comes from the Latin *credo*—"I believe." Someone has faith in us or this little piece of plastic would lose its magic. The credit card comes from the same Latin word that gives us *creed*. We speak the creed of our religious faith at our place of worship, and we count on the creed of our financial faith each time we use the credit card. Faith is so woven into our living that we rarely notice its manifestations even while we're walking through them.

Until now I've mentioned only the commonplace areas of faith. But what shall I say about those profound expressions of faith that are the very heartbeat of our lives? What about the faith we have in coworkers, friends, and family members? We bet our happiness, our emotional security, and sometimes our very lives on the faith we have in people. Most of us have seen that faith betrayed at some point in our lives, and we've probably done our own share of betraying, ranging all the way from the kindergarten playground to a cherished friendship, a marriage, or a business partner. Nevertheless, most of us don't stop believing in people after we've had such an experience, and we feel sorry for anyone who allows such a breach of trust to turn them into a miscreant. We *want* to believe. Thus someone says after a shattering violation of friendship, "What I hate most is that I'm afraid I'll never be able to trust anyone again." The loss or the diminishing of the ability to believe in people is even greater than the loss of the particular relationship.

This is the stuff we human beings are made of. This is one of the signal elements that makes us human. We are not only rational creatures, creating creatures, and decision makers; we are *believers*.

When the book of Genesis tells us about Adam and Eve's dialogue with the serpent, the ultimate issue is a matter of faith—in this case, a matter of misplaced faith. They chose to trust in the counsel of the serpent rather than to believe in God. It was at this point that we humans lost our innocence. And it isn't surprising that Adam and Eve then hid from God, because once their faith was shattered (even if by a deceiving intruder) it made them doubt any authority. To doubt is to fear, so they wanted now to avoid God. Nor is it surprising that they began to distrust each other; thus Adam, who had been so pleased to have Eve, started complaining to God about Eve's misleading him. And we shouldn't be surprised when we learn that Adam and Eve were cast out of the perfection of Eden, because to lose faith is to lose paradise. Just ask any disillusioned romantic.

Faith is an essential element in living. Without it, we can't get along with others and we can't get along with ourselves. If we doubt others, we withdraw from them, even if we remain physically present. We can become antisocial even while engaging in social discourse. If we lose faith in ourselves we become our own ever-present, inescapable enemies. I agree with the Apostle Paul when he says that faith, hope, and love abide and that the greatest of these is love; but love itself depends so often on the faith we have in the object of our love and in the degree to which we trust our judgment in loving.

If faith is such an essential factor in life, and if furthermore it is such a normal part of our human equipment, how is it that when we need faith the most, we can't seem to get it? If faith is such a constant factor in our daily living, why do we find it hard to exercise faith where it matters most, in our dealings with God? And if faith is so important in getting along with people, in living with ourselves, and in knowing God and thus in enjoying life, how can we get more faith? Or how can we put our faith to work in those areas of life where it matters most, and at the times when we need it most?

For answers I turn to the finest short essay on faith to be found anywhere. You will find it in a New Testament book titled the Letter to the Hebrews. We don't know for sure who wrote this book. Most of the Epistles—letters—in the New Testament have a name attached to them, much like a letterhead on a piece of stationery, but this one moves right into its business without even a word of greeting. Nor do we know the exact date when it was written, although it was probably around the year 65.

It's easy to see why this letter was written. Some Christians in that long-ago time were losing faith ("losing heart," some would call it), and the unknown author wanted to restore it. Because of the nature of his pleading—his careful, extensive references to the teachings of the Hebrew Scriptures—many assume that he was writing to Jewish Christians, thus the title that was given to the letter, a letter that is really more like a sermon.

The letter comes to a powerful climax in chapter 11. You can read this chapter in less time than it takes to read a newspaper account of yesterday's football game, and at times it moves in the same kind of breathtaking style so that you want to say, "I wish I'd been there to see it for myself." And at about that time the writer indicates that the game of faith—all the accumulated centuries of it—was played for your benefit, so that now the people who brought the game to this point are waiting to see what you will do with the continuing competition. You discover that you've moved from a seat in the stands to a place on the playing field. You started your reading as a spectator and now you're a key participant, and the people who began the game are now cheering you on.

I should have warned you that faith is like that. You can't spend your life viewing it from a distance. At some point you're compelled to be part of the action. That's because faith is woven into the fabric of our lives. Reading the eleventh chapter of Hebrews is something like attending one of those dinner theaters where they're performing a murder mystery and suddenly they make the audience part of the play, drafting them as witnesses to the crime.

It reminds me of a noted newspaper writer from the early twentieth century who said that Jesus was no doubt a very fine gentleman but that he, the newspaper writer, preferred not to be involved but to remain an innocent bystander. The writer of Hebrews won't let us be innocent bystanders. Faith isn't that kind of game, and we aren't that kind of creature. From what I know about angels, they may have a kind of bystander role because they don't seem to have any faith issues. But you and I, we humans, were made for faith, and the ultimate issue of our existence is the battle between faith and unbelief.

Not faith and doubt, mind you. These two are not opposites. Doubt is a way station en route to faith. I can't imagine getting to faith at a grand level that raises the hair on your arms without passing through doubt to get there. If I may change the figure of speech, faith is an edifice in which some of the grandest parts are the various stones and mortar of doubt. Don't worry about doubt. Doubt is the stuff that goes into the building of faith.

Unbelief is another matter. Unbelief sets itself against faith and is determined not to give it a hearing. Unbelief grows nervous in the presence of faith because it knows that if it stays around long enough, it will lose. It's an unfair battle, you see, because, as I mentioned earlier, you and I are made for faith, so unbelief is always an intruder, always working against what is magnificently native to us. As that fine eighteenth-century poet William Cowper wrote: "Blind unbelief is sure to err / and scan God's work in vain."[1] Cowper knew from experience. He was a person often given to struggles with deep depression, so he wrestled many a pitched battle with unbelief. But he learned repeatedly that unbelief is sure to err.

As for doubting, it shouldn't be seen as a destination, but it has its place. There are some who find a kind of intellectual pride in doubting, suggesting that their doubts demonstrate the superior quality of their thinking. Not so. They may be demonstrating instead an unwillingness to come to a conclusion. Doubts are for the soul what a failed experiment is to the scientist; they represent a temporary delay in reaching the goal. The Spanish philosopher and essayist Miguel de Unamuno put it this way: "A faith which does not doubt is a dead faith."[2] I don't want to put words in Unamuno's mouth, but as I see it, faith is a live and growing thing precisely because it is always contending with new areas of doubt.

We will see as we travel through the faith hall of fame that is given to us in Hebrews 11 that these exemplars of faith were also able doubters. Fortunately for us the writer of this Christian epistle, like the writers of the Hebrew Scriptures before him, wasn't afraid to be honest. These biblical writers didn't feel that God was in any way diminished by our human uncertainties. To the contrary, the faith position is all the better and all the more authentic for the struggles that lead to it. Faith is not a hothouse plant, protected from the elements, but rather jungle wild, finding its quality in the issues that we think might destroy it.

Nor is faith the exclusive position of saints. Saints don't make faith; but faith when it has its perfect work makes saints. As I read about the lives of great souls, some of whom have been identified by the Catholic Church as saints and some of whom are recognized simply by the common assent of the rest of us, I find that many of them are in holy combat to the day of death. This is because they have kept growing and have continually found new areas of spiritual conquest. Some of the noblest have lived through periods that they describe as "the dark night of the soul." And though in their struggle God has sometimes seemed far distant, they were in truth drawing closest to their Lord.

There are also persons who cannot be classified as conventional believers who nevertheless demonstrate remarkable faith at some particular time. I think of King Cyrus, a powerful man who had gods of his own. But "the LORD stirred up the spirit of King Cyrus" (Ezra 1:1) so that Cyrus made it possible for the Jewish captives to return to their homeland. For that circumstance he became a believer, and believed deeply enough to be radically generous and to deal repeatedly with resistance from Israel's enemies. Some of Jesus' most notable miracles were for faith's outsiders—like the centurion who sought healing for his servant. "Lord, I am not worthy to have you come under my roof," he explained; and Jesus marveled that this man with no evident spiritual heritage showed more faith than people who enjoyed a heritage in Judaism (Matthew 8:5-13).

Nor is this kind of faith from beyond the borders limited to Bible times. Herman Melville was not a conventionally religious man, but I can find no stronger case for preaching than in his description of the power of the pulpit in his novel *Moby Dick*. John Steinbeck would probably be classified an agnostic, but in his novel *East of Eden* he wrestles with the issue of sin in biblical language more effectively than it has been done in most sermons I've heard. Often I read lines of quite secular poems that speak faith eloquently while the poet dwells in unbelief. When the nineteenth-century English poet Francis Thompson describes his flight from God in "The Hound of Heaven," he seems to recite the story of our human race in its fascination with faith in the midst of humanity's worst unbelief.

So it is that we begin our look at faith from the back side. Faith is part of our original human equipment, older than anything read or written. Nevertheless, it is our most embattled virtue, more difficult to hold onto than love. We exercise faith every day, in hundreds of secular moments, then struggle to find it in its purest form when we need God's help the most. The back side, indeed! Sometimes it's the only side we can seem to approach. Yet faith is nearer than our hands or feet and more real than the air we breathe.

It's time we learned more about it from a great, anonymous, first-century believer who was trying to help friends who thought their faith was almost gone. So it is that we go now to the eleventh chapter of Hebrews.

CHAPTER TWO

Faith Has an Attitude

Scripture Reading: Hebrews 11:1-2

Faith has an attitude. I'm using that term in the way you see it on the sports page when coaches or sports analysts say of certain athletes that they carry themselves with "an attitude"—that is, that they perform with a quality of such assured confidence that at times it may even seem like a strut. At its best there's nothing of arrogance in it, just the calm assurance that the athlete knows he or she is equipped to win. Their natural gifts and their preparation for contest make winning seem not simply possible but almost certain.

In the world of the spirit this is the attitude of those who choose to trust in God and in the promises of God. This doesn't mean that they're naive about the conflict in which they're engaged; generally, they're experienced warriors. They have a proper sense of the factors aligned against them: they know that the culture in which they live is probably unsympathetic to the purposes of God, and they know that sometimes the attitudes of the people around them—those people who expect defeat as surely as the faithful expect victory—can be enervating. And of course they know themselves well enough to know something about the problems within their own persons—the unevenness that comes within the workings of one's mind and spirit. They also know something about those elements that are our declared enemies—what the Apostle Paul refers to as "the cosmic powers of this present darkness . . . the spiritual forces of evil in the heavenly places" (Ephesians 6:12). The faith-person knows that any number of factors are marshaled in opposition. But the faith-person expects to win—not because the enemy is weak, but because faith's resources are substantially greater than the best of those that can be brought against him or her.

The faith-person knows particularly that the primary issue is not the quality of his or her trust in God, but rather the attitude God has toward us. That's part of what I have in mind when I speak of the back side of faith, and it is essential to the way we define and exercise faith in our daily living. I shall return to this later.

Eugene Peterson's translation says, "The act of faith is what distinguished our ancestors, set them above the crowd" (Hebrews 11:2 *THE MESSAGE*). "Our ancestors" refers of course to our spiritual ancestors, as recited for us in the eleventh chapter of Hebrews. (And for you and me, living twenty centuries later, it includes the additional faith-giants who have appeared in every generation of Christ's followers.) These faith-ancestors possessed that special something that "set them above the crowd"—the crowd in every generation that seems content to live in the lowlands of life. Our spiritual ancestors had nothing if not *attitude*.

They often embarrassed their friends and supporters; they irritated their enemies; they got themselves in endless trouble; and they scared the hell out of hell.

This attitude begins with definitions. These definitions are worked out not in a library or a philosophical discussion, worthy as those settings often are. They are definitions from the battlefield, or, if you prefer, from the laboratory. In any event, they have been put to the test not as controlled experiments, and not as preseason exhibition games, but at those places where the conflict counts, often as a life-and-death matter and always as an eternal matter. This is part of the nature of faith; it takes hold of life at its eternal point, realizing that all of life has a peculiar, insistent eternal quality. And there's still more to it. The faith-person comes to realize that all of life is affected by our faith decisions—not simply the choices we make at the altar of Communion or dedication, but both the excitement and the humdrum of daily living. The faith-person sees all of life through faith, and takes all of life dominion for God and God's purpose. Thus while we may not consciously list our definitions as faith-actions, they include our understanding of God, of ourselves, of life and its greater meaning, and of what we think life should give us.

The classic language of the King James Version defines faith this way: "Faith is the substance of things hoped for, the evidence of things not seen" (Hebrews 11:1 KJV). This is an attitude toward life, and it is one that runs counter to our usual definitions. Sometimes as I read that verse I'm not sure whether the writer was writing a Magna Carta declaration for hell or whether he was being playful, expecting that his readers would see the humor in what he was saying. After all, "substance" is usually seen as something we can lay our hands on. Faith finds its substance in "things *hoped for.*" Things "hoped for" are the opposite of "substance." Is the writer of Hebrews delivering this idea with a wink and a grin?

Such is also the case with "evidence." The dictionary defines *evidence* as "ground for belief; that which tends to prove or disprove something." "Ground for belief" conveys the sense of something we can stand on. But the writer of Hebrews tells us that faith is "the evidence of things not seen." What kind of evidence do I bring to court in "things not seen"? If evidence is "ground for belief," how is it that it leads us into "things not seen"? And how does one stand on such ground as this? Pretty clearly this first-century Christian has an attitude. He doesn't mind using words in ways contrary to our usual conceptions.

The writer of Hebrews got this attitude from Jesus. Consider the scene in Matthew 17. Jesus was with Peter, James, and John on "a high mountain" when suddenly "he was transfigured before them"; and while "his face shone like the sun, and his clothes became dazzling white" Moses and Elijah joined them, talking with Jesus (vv. 1-3). It was an ecstatic experience for the disciples; but as they returned to the other disciples and an assembled crowd at the foot of the mountain, they were—to use a common expression—"brought down to earth."

Because there Jesus was greeted by a heartbroken father. His son was severely afflicted with epilepsy. In hope, the father had brought him to the disciples, "but they could not cure him"

(Matthew 17:16). I wonder what excuse or explanation the disciples gave the man. I don't want to treat them unsympathetically because I suspect I would have felt equally helpless if I had been in their place.

But there's no question how Jesus felt. His sympathies were all with the father, and for the disciples he had nothing but holy impatience: "How much longer must I put up with you?" (v. 17). Jesus was sick of the lack of faith he saw in these people who were with him daily, hearing his teaching and seeing his miracles. He called them a "faithless and perverse generation" (v. 17)—that is, Jesus saw their lack of faith as a *perverse* quality, a state of mind and conduct in opposition to God's will. And here is a lesson for us: a lack of faith in God is not simply a void in our lives; it is a *perverse* attitude toward God and toward all that life should be. Jesus then proceeded to heal the boy; he was "cured instantly" (v. 18).

I'll say this for the disciples: they wanted to do better. They weren't content with themselves as they were. So they asked Jesus his secret. Why couldn't they do what he had just done? Clearly it wasn't some magic formula. I suspect that when the father and the boy came to the disciples the disciples spoke some of the same prayers and declarations they had heard Jesus use on other occasions with similar needs. How is it that the language didn't work for them, that their prayers were ineffective? What was their lack?

Jesus' answer was direct and clear: "Because you have little faith." Then he let them know precisely how he evaluated their faith: "I assure you that if you have faith the size of a mustard

14

seed, you could say to this mountain, 'Go from here to there,' and it will go. There will be nothing that you can't do" (Matthew 17:20-21 CEB).

That, I repeat, is an attitude. To put it again in the language of sports, this is the football player who says on the fourth down, with the time clock running out and the game on the line, "Give me the ball!" The disciples asked, "Why can't we win this battle with hell?" And Jesus replied, "How can you help but win? If you had even a smidgeon of faith, faith like that mustard seed that can get lost in the deep groove of a laboring man's hand, you could do anything."

But godly faith is not open to superficial interpretations. See what follows. Jesus tells his disciples that he is on his way to betrayal, and that he will be killed, and that "on the third day he will be raised" (Matthew 17:22-23). It's interesting that this statement about Jesus' death and resurrection follows so soon after the promise that nothing is impossible for his followers if only they have faith. If faith is so powerful, couldn't they do something to prevent their Lord's betrayal or to combat those who would kill him? And if they had a sense of those who were opposing Jesus, I wonder if it seemed to the disciples that they should have been able by faith to deal with such opposition.

The quality of faith is such, however, that it doesn't need to win each skirmish along the way. Often enough some of those battles are lost. What shall we say of the millions who have suffered martyrdom over the twenty centuries of church history? What shall we say of those times when evil has clearly been in the ascendancy and faith and truth have been driven into corners of defeat? We shall say what those martyrs have said by their dying: "The body they may kill; / God's truth abideth still; / his kingdom is forever."[1] As Hugh Latimer said to Bishop Ridley as they were about to be burned at the stake in Oxford, England, on October 16, 1555: "Be of good comfort, Master Ridley, and play the man. We shall this day light such a candle, by God's grace, in England, as I trust shall never be put out."[2]

That's what I mean by *attitude*. There's a swagger to that that makes the flames look foolish. There's a mustard seed that threatens hell. Faith knows it cannot ultimately lose. Case closed. And by the way, the disciples learned this so well that according to tradition all but the Apostle John died by martyrdom—winning.

As we make our way through the eleventh chapter of Hebrews we will see this kind of faith again and again. It is faith that cannot lose. In the Old Testament account, as the book of Hebrews recalls it, the cause of faith is often buried and then suddenly discovered to be as alive as ever. Faith doesn't know when the battle is lost. So it is that Abel suffers an untimely death but is the carrier still of hope and honor. Noah belongs to a miniscule minority in his day, yet he wins. Watch him build his ark, and see his attitude! Abraham and Sarah are called to a new life when their age suggests they should be retiring in a more accommodating climate; instead, they march! Rahab is a harlot, a figure living on the outskirts of respectability even in a carnal culture. But she has an attitude—faith in a God from beyond her language and culture, and faith that makes her put her life on the line. And lo and behold, we find her name in the New Testament as an ancestress to our Lord Jesus Christ.

Those who walk by faith learn that you don't have to win today's election, ball game, corporate merger, or dormitory room argument. Sometimes, as you learn later, it's just as well that you didn't. But faith knows that you can't lose, and that gives you an attitude—a calm assurance; a glad excitement in living or in dying; an "It is well with my soul" and "O Love that wilt not let me go" and "Lord, we are able." Living or dying, seeming to win or seeming to lose, the attitude is the same. "Substance" or "hoped for," "evidence" or "not seen," seems to make no difference.

Now this is a decidedly "back side" way of approaching life. Mind you, I hasten to add, it is a very exciting way, but nevertheless back side. As far as the writer of Hebrews is concerned, however, it is the only way, and he leads us through centuries of faith history to prove it. And we sense as we read that the "for instances" are really the definition. They give us examples so we will understand how the somewhat self-contradictory definition of faith looks when we see it in action. Faith is a story woven out in the lives of people. And they are people we know—not because we have met them physically but because they fill some empty pages in the album of our spiritual family. They show us that while faith is reasonable to those who understand it, it is not a reasoned document but a collection of insistent realities.

I want again to remind us that in its raw state faith is not exclusively a matter of belief in God. Indeed, human faith chooses the gods in which it will invest itself. And it is proper enough that we humans invest faith in all of the business of living: in people; in ideas; in work and culture and aspirations. We must use faith in this practical fashion in order to live. The difference for the writer of Hebrews and for Scripture as a whole is that the ultimate focus of our faith—the focus that determines all the rest of our faith investment—is in God as revealed to us in Jesus Christ. Thus Oscar Blackwelder, a fine preacher-scholar in the mid-twentieth century, says of the scientist, "Every hypothesis is a practice of faith; all science rests upon faith." Blackwelder then goes on to note that in the moral and spiritual world the same process exists. He continues: "The man of Christian faith takes Christ as his hypothesis, his postulate, his most glorious thesis."[3] The people to whom the book of Hebrews was written had so taken Christ. Now they had to bet their very lives on what they believed, and the writer of Hebrews assures them that they have made the right choice.

Earlier in this chapter I said that the primary issue with faith is not the quality of our trust in God but rather the attitude God has toward us. You and I are remarkably made. The psalmist said in his worship of God, "Yet you have made them [humans] a little lower than God, / and crowned them with glory and honor" (Psalm 8:5). We've been given dominion, he writes, over the works of God's hands. We are, so to speak, a valuable property. Our capacity for life is unfathomable. This is why the misuse of our minds and personalities and skill sets is nothing short of blasphemous. And this is why it is so heinous for us to be drugged into a sodden state, whether by chemical substance, sexual addiction, cheap ambition, ennui, self-absorption, or the intellectual stupor caused by too much television and Internet. This kind of drugging keeps us from fulfilling our potential as human beings— the potential God has invested in us.

The best reason you and I have for faith in God is the faith God has in us. You and I are so singularly made because God has singular expectations for us. You and I need to have an attitude toward life because of the attitude God has toward us. There's a strut and a swagger in that scene in the opening chapter of Genesis where God finished making the human creature—"in the image of God he created them; / male and female he created them"—and then blessed us and contemplated all we would do (Genesis 1:26-30). And looking at it—looking at *us*—God saw that "indeed, it was very good" (Genesis 1:31).

When God finished you and me, it was with an attitude—a grand confidence. If God has such faith in us, how dare we have a fumbling faith in God?

CHAPTER THREE

Faith Has a History

Scripture Reading: Hebrews 11:3

Sin has a long history. Someone has noted that in the average Bible the reader has only reached page three when sin appears. "Original sin" is a theological term, but it has a kind of philosophical tilt as if sin is uncomfortably close to our origins, or perhaps it's the first original thing we humans did. Even if you don't think of sin as being the most original thing about us—and if you do, I want to change your thinking—in truth, sin has a long history. And when we humans try to grapple with sin seriously, we sometimes feel we're involved in a doomed conflict because sin was here before we were and thus it knows the territory and the contours of battle in ways we don't. It seems, therefore, that we can hardly hope to hold our own against it.

But I submit that however old sin may be, faith is older. And if the history of sin is a discouraging fact, the history of faith is a dramatic rebuttal to anything sin may try to say.

The eleventh chapter of the New Testament book of Hebrews is a faith tour de force that is intended to build faith in us. It is told through vignettes from biblical history and from the inter-testamental period and from the book of 2 Maccabees. And after defining faith, where does the writer begin his recital of this whole grand story? "By faith we understand that the worlds were prepared by the word of God, so that what is seen was made from things that are not visible" (Hebrews 11:3). It begins with the creation.

The unspoken inference is clear. If you're talking about faith, you're talking about something so old that the only proper place to begin the discussion is at the *beginning*. Faith is as old as the human story. No, it is older than that; it was here to greet us humans when we arrived.

The Bible explains that it is "by faith we understand" the creation. I think that the most devout readers of the Bible should realize better than anyone that we grasp the creation story not by particular evidences of science or logic, but by faith. We rejoice in that fact. I don't mean to disparage science or those who place the Scriptures in an argument with natural science. I want sim-ply to say that the ultimate response to creation is in a hymn of adoration. We join chorus with the psalmist when he exults: "The heavens are telling the glory of God; / and the firmament proclaims his handiwork" (Psalm 19:1).

It is more than that. The writer of Hebrews is confessing that the creation story is hard to believe. You must approach creation from a posture of faith if you are to grasp it. Genesis tells us that God *spoke*, and things happened: light, separation of water from land, the beginning of vegetation, creatures of air and sea and land—always by the formula "And God said." The New

Testament Gospel of John uses the same dramatic and audacious language: "In the beginning was the Word," and it was by this Word that "all things came into being" (John 1:1, 3). And of course the writer of Hebrews uses the same kind of language: "The worlds were prepared *by the word of God*" (Hebrews 11:3; emphasis added).

The biblical story would have been much easier to accept if it had shown God as a Master Architect or the Ultimate Engineer, working with the original slide rule or some heavenly computer. Indeed, we might find the account more acceptable if it showed God organizing parts both large and small, shaping atoms in the divine hand and counting out particles like an accountant. We like it when the prophet Isaiah says of God: "Who has measured the waters in the hollow of his hand / and marked off the heavens with a span?" (Isaiah 40:12). This is poetic enough to satisfy the imagination and physical enough to suggest logic. But the biblical creation story compels us to a full faith leap: God *spoke*, and it happened. It is as if the Scriptures left us no alternative: read with faith. Read with imagination, perhaps; with adoration, of course; but with faith, absolutely.

But there is yet more. Is the biblical writer telling us that God was working with faith in the creation process? Was the very act of creation a work of divine faith? Is this part of the inference in the opening verses of Genesis when we're told that "when God created the heavens and the earth, the earth was a formless void and darkness covered the face of the deep" (Genesis 1:1-2)? The Hebrew scholar Robert Alter translates "formless void" as "welter and waste" and reminds us that the first word (Hebrew *tohu*) by itself means "futility, emptiness."[1] In other words, it's a pretty dismal scene; not much reason here for hope. When we look at such "futility" it's hard to imagine the beauty of a rose opening or the song of a bird, to say nothing of the precision of the planets.

I am not suggesting that God felt seriously challenged by the problems of creation or that the divine mind had to work overtime some days in order to deal with the welter and waste. I am suggesting that the biblical writer wants us to know that the creation was a grand achievement, starting as it did with "a formless void and darkness." And perhaps, even, Genesis wants us to understand that God was operating with faith in the process of creation.

Does it seem inappropriate to think of God having *faith*? In *what*? one wants to ask. In what or in whom does God have faith? Well, the Scriptures tell us that God is *love* (1 John 4:16), and that "love is from God," and that "everyone who loves is born of God" (1 John 4:7). So why should we hesitate to relate faith to God? Certainly we can be sure that faith comes from God, just as love does. Perhaps we understand God better if we see God doing the eternal work by faith, by eternal confidence in the divine purposes. Was God the Creator confronted by welter and waste? And does that suggest that faith will always have to deal with welter and waste? Certainly God has been confronted by a good deal of our human welter and waste through the centuries since creation.

Let's take still another look at the way Hebrews unfolds this story of faith at work. The writer tells us that "what is seen was made from things that are not visible" (Hebrews 11:3). This is the language we find in the previous verse, which defines faith as "the conviction of things not seen." The creation process was the essence of faith. Like faith, which is based on "things not seen," the creation process itself "was made from things that are not visible."

I don't look to science to prove or disprove my understanding of creation. I admit readily that I am not a scientist and that my knowledge in this field is meager, far behind my knowledge of literature, history, and religion. I read the creation story in Genesis, with its later "commentaries" in the Psalms and Hebrews and the Gospel of John, as an act of communion with God and with a desire to know God better. But while I don't ask science to "prove" Genesis, and while for me it cannot disprove Genesis (primarily because science and Genesis are working on two different formats), I am fascinated by a similarity in perception at one point. Professor Ursula Goodenough, one of America's leading cell biologists, says that our "observable universe is about fifteen billion years old. In the beginning, everything that is now that universe, including all of its space, was concentrated in a singularity, maybe the size of a pinhead."[2] The size of a pinhead! That gives me the same feeling as Hebrews' statement that the creation "was made from things that are not visible."

So I approach creation with the sublime faith that God is its ultimate origin, whatever the process, and that therefore God has a purpose in it—a purpose that reassures my entire attitude toward life and living. Moreover, I believe that God went about the creation process with faith as surely as with love. When Genesis tells us that early in the process of creation there was "futility" and "emptiness," I think it might be telling us that we should never be disheartened by our occasional and unpredictable confrontations with such conditions. We should approach them as God approached such a scene while bringing our universe into existence: with faith.

One more word about faith as part of the creation process: at each juncture in the creation process we're told that God "saw that it was good." I don't want to press language too far because language always has its limits, especially when we use language (as we must) in trying to describe God and God's work in our world, but when Genesis tells us of God's pleasure in each step of creation, it has the mood of "This has worked out just as I planned it"—that is, the quality of faith fulfilled.

So faith has a history. It isn't a newcomer to the human neighborhood. It was here before we moved in! When the New Testament writer wants to tell us the grandeur of the procession we're joining when we become part of the company of faith, he offers us an impressive line from our human ancestors, dating all the way back to a noble man, Abel—the first martyr. (And isn't it interesting that the Bible presents us with a martyr so early in the human story and that this martyr was a person of faith—the first person so identified.)

But the writer knew that he couldn't begin the faith story with any human being, not even one as admirable as Abel. He takes us all the way back to creation—something we accept in faith but also something that was by its nature a venture in faith.

Thus when you and I act in faith—specifically, faith in God rather than faith in general—we are in line with the way our universe is made. As surely as our universe operates with principles of love and justice and purity, it operates also with faith. When we believe, we are in line with the way our universe is made. We are in true, divine harmony with creation.

Our whole outlook on life rests in large measure on how we view our universe. If we see it as happening by chance and as existing with no particular purpose, then our own individual lives take on the same character. We then see life as a void (welter and waste!) and our participation in it as a rather meaningless charade, one in which we perform as best we can but feel that it's never much more than a parlor game. But if we believe that our universe itself is an expression of God's faith—God's grand, ultimately indomitable purpose—then you and I are creatures of purpose and meaning as well. In fact, as caretakers of what is, to our knowledge, the only inhabited part of this universe, we have an assignment quite beyond comprehension. We are subcreators, contributing to the continuing creative process. When we accept our universe with faith, we sign on to carry the faith process into its divine purpose.

This brings us to our role as subcreators. In a sense, "subcreator" is a contradiction in terms, because when we use the term *create* in the Genesis way, we are speaking of creating out of nothing. Anything we humans create is created out of something already in existence. For the scientist creation comes from mathematical formulae that go back all the way to the first time someone counted from one to three; for the composer it comes from the time someone first appreciated the gradations of sound; and for the literary artist creation comes from the first time someone first sensed a lovelier, more persuasive way to put three words together. Anyone who creates in any field works with something (by this twenty-first century, with many things!) that has been given to us from the past. And for a person with any sense of the divine, the "past" goes back to God.

J. R. R. Tolkien, whose imaginative tales have attracted a larger audience than ever in recent years, felt that we humans are always only subcreators and that all stories originate with God. His friend and fellow "Inkling" C. S. Lewis concurred. "All stories," Lewis said, "are waiting, somewhere, and are slowly being recovered in fragments by different human minds according to their abilities—and of course being partially spoiled in each writer by the admixture of his own mere individual 'invention.'"[3]

I like that very much. I like the feeling that you and I are part of a grand procession of creators, beneficiaries of a fathomless store of knowledge and beauty upon which we can draw if we are sensitive enough (and humble enough) to tap in. And I am very sure that Lewis is right when he says that in some measure we spoil whatever we get "by the admixture of [our] own mere individual 'invention.'" In a sense, that's what leaves something for another person—another generation—to find and to improve.

This creative impulse is fascinating to observe. A preschool child makes a statement or asks a question that seems to come out of nowhere, and a grown-up says, "Where did she come up with that?" and perhaps looks at the parents and thinks that the child couldn't have gotten it from her mother or father! But of course the mother or father's creativity, whatever its original quality, has been tamed by years of television and by the isolation that comes with making a living or a career.

In some areas of life creativity has been accelerated in the past half century to a degree that is breathtaking. Ironically, our new discoveries, arts, and inventions seem often to make necessary still other research and discovery. Some of our achievements open the door for new problems. A healing medicine becomes for some a compulsive drug; a new chemical is for a rising tyrant a way of bringing other nations under his control. Sometimes the genius of a composer or a playwright becomes a distraction that keeps susceptible minds from doing their work or caring for those who depend on them. So it is that we must keep creating in order to cope with our own handiwork.

We are creators—subcreators—no doubt about it. That part of our genetic code—the divine part—makes us so. It gifts us whether we acknowledge it or not, and deserve it or not, and whether we will use it, abuse it, or allow it to lie in neglect.

We need these creative souls; we need them in a life-and-death way. We need them to find answers to cancer, arthritis, diabetes, Alzheimer's, AIDS, muscular dystrophy, multiple sclerosis, Lou Gehrig's disease, and diseases yet unknown or not yet diagnosed. We need poets, novelists, preachers, and playwrights who can help us laugh with depth, cry with sympathy and understanding, and think with passion. And we need creative geniuses in the world of politics and economics so that injustice and poverty will be made as nearly obsolete as human effort can manage.

When a new creative star appears on the literary or musical scene, critics try to find a comparison. The best critics generally reach back a ways into the giants in the field. I read a novel recently that a thoughtful critic compared to the work of Mark Twain. I heard a concert where a new composer was compared cautiously to Mozart.

The devout, at such times, will pause and thank God for the gift of creativity and for God's generosity in dispensing this gift with us humans in such prodigal fashion. "By faith we understand that the worlds were prepared by the word of God, so that what is seen was made from things that are not visible."

I cannot see a more profound solution for poverty, cure for the deadliest and ugliest of afflictions, or new loveliness of symphony or of language. But I believe that faith is older than all our problems and more profound than all our best longings, and I believe that the God who created is at the desk of creation still. And I hope that by faith you and I can be subcreators in God's continuing work with the welter and waste of our wayward planet.

CHAPTER FOUR

Faith Sometimes Walks, Sometimes Flies

Scripture Reading: Hebrews 11:4-6

Faith has so many faces. On any given day we're likely to have faith encounters at a hundred different corners. Most of the time we pass by these meetings without even a courteous nod of the soul. A few moments more and we have lost the face of faith in the panorama of matters large and small. The people we call saints are different—and that's why we call them saints. They are more sensitive to the occasions of faith visits than most of us are, so they have them more often. If you and I would develop better spiritual vision there's no imagining how many times we might see the face of faith in the daily crowd of vague images.

Let me start with the story of the two fabled brothers Cain and Abel. Cain had a head start to significance not only because he was born first but also because his mother, Eve, had such high hopes for him. She named him "Produced," or "Gotten," because she said, "I have produced a man with the help of the LORD"

(Genesis 4:1). There's no such excitement with the birth of the younger brother, Abel. The writer of Genesis says simply, almost laconically, "Next she bore his brother Abel" (4:2). There is no particular significance in his name, and his only identifying label is via his relationship to his older brother.

When others have high expectations for us it's a burden, but a rather nice one. It's much better, at any rate, than when people say, "You'll never amount to much," or when they simply notice us only incidentally because we're tagging along with those who are more important. You know what I mean. It's like when someone reports on a social occasion with mention of the two or three memorable persons and you ask, "Was Sally there by any chance?" and the other party replies, "Oh, yes, I forgot to mention that Sally was there too." Abel was there too, in the family of Adam and Eve, but all eyes were on Cain—especially the eyes of his mother.

The boys grew up and found their respective careers, Abel as a keeper of sheep and Cain as a tiller of the soil. Both are honorable occupations, both depend on the vagaries of nature, and both have their share of routine, tiring labor. The classic language that refers to these occupations as "animal husbandry" and "plant husbandry" is well chosen because you're compelled to marry this kind of work. And odds are strong that you will feel a particular dependence on God. You may refer to God in vague references to nature, but you know that try as you will, your efforts can be thwarted by too little or too much rain or by some errant disease that wipes out half of your flock. Thus it's no wonder that Cain and Abel celebrated harvest time by bringing an offering to the Lord.

That's when Cain—the ranked one, the especially beloved, the one with high expectations—got a shock. I don't know how often, if ever, Cain had experienced coming in second. We know for sure that he was born first and that his mother expected him to remain first; but as Cain and Abel stood before the Lord, Cain ran a quite dismal second. If Abel's offering had pleased God and Cain's had run a close second it would have been hard enough for this born achiever Cain. But it was worse: "And the LORD had regard for Abel and his offering, but for Cain and his offering he had no regard" (Genesis 4:4-5).

This is a harsh word, and it's hard to understand unless you go on to the New Testament to read a divine commentary on the scene via the book of Hebrews. There the issue is spelled out clearly. "By faith Abel offered to God a more acceptable sacrifice than Cain's. Through this he received approval as righteous, God himself giving approval to his gifts" (Hebrews 11:4).

The difference between Cain and Abel? Faith.

Is there any substantive evidence of this difference in the Genesis story? Professor Robert Alter suggests that it may be indicated in the fact that "Abel brings the very best of his flock to God"—"the choice firstlings of his flock," as Alter translates it.[1]

This phrase suggests that Abel's offering was no incidental choice; he sought out the best that he had so he could use it for his sacrifice. Such effort is indeed an act of faith. There's nothing casual about faith. It is a choice from the soul, and often a very difficult one, though it's likely to become easier over time.

There is other evidence, in the Genesis story, of Cain's lack of faith, and it helps us in our definition of faith. When Cain realized that God had responded unfavorably to his offering he "was very angry, and his countenance fell" (Genesis 4:5). Now a person in a peevish pique is uniquely unappealing; nevertheless, God solicited Cain, which, let me say, is a quite impressive expression of grace early in the biblical story. Like a parent seeking out a pouting child, God asks the reason for Cain's anger. After all, the situation was in Cain's control: if you do well, you'll be accepted, God explains, and if not, "sin is lurking at the door." And most important of all, God assures Cain that he "must master it" (Genesis 4:7). As we know, Cain chose instead to be rid of his brother.

The story shows us that faith is an attitude of the mind and that in time that mental attitude will show itself in physical deeds—in the case of Cain, by the act of assault and murder. If we give faith a chance it shows us where we fall short; moreover, it empowers us to change our ways. Thus we learn that faith is far more than a pleasant feeling of well-being or of high expectation. Faith is a power that brings change in the life and thinking of the person who allows it to work. It stirs the conscience so that we have the incentive and the courage to confront our failures. Thus when we pray for faith the answer may come not in a miracle of pleasure ("God has accepted my sacrifice!") but in a new depth of character by which we take better control of our lives. The miracle that follows will seem to some to be no miracle at all but simply a matter of us becoming persons who take charge.

Cain, a person who lacked faith, has an important faith lesson for us. The first step of faith is the willingness to examine our conduct and our thinking in order to see where we've gone wrong or how we might do better. It is the faith in knowing that we can change and that very possibly we ought to do so. It is, in other words, an act of humility. This shouldn't surprise us. After all, faith in God is always an acknowledgement that we need help from beyond ourselves. Well, the first such step is to know where we are at fault or where our thinking may be in error. Thus the best lesson you and I can learn from Cain and his lack of faith is to seek the courage to face our own person with an open mind and a humble, willing heart.

As for Abel, what did faith do for him? For what achievement do we remember him? What waters of the sea does he push back? What lions does he confront in their den? In truth, his life ends with nothing more than a first good year as a herdsman and the declaration that he won God's favor. His life seems to belong to that group we describe as never coming to fulfillment. "He had so much promise," we say, "but his life was cut short."

But the writer of Hebrews sees it otherwise and uses Abel as the first human "for instance" in his catalog of faith. Abel's brief faith biography concludes, "He died, but through his faith he still speaks" (Hebrews 11:4). This shouldn't surprise us. All of us know of persons—sometimes famous, sometimes known only to an intimate circle—who died in an attempt to protect someone else or in loyalty to a cause but who are legendary in their dying.

Abel's story also tells us, very early in this faith chapter, that death is not the worst thing that can happen. As a villain, death has been overrated. In the popular recasting of Tertullian's words at the turn of the third century, "The blood of the martyrs is the seed of the Church."[2] I remember a young man only a few years my senior who died at Guadalcanal because—as his superior reported it—he volunteered for an assignment that would almost certainly be fatal. Nearly seventy years later he still speaks to me. I don't know if the military decision that led to his death was correct; I do know that ultimately war itself is a flawed enterprise. But I also know the courage that drove my friend (it was consistent with who he was), and I know that he still speaks.

Another lesson from faith's back side: we don't have to win every game. Some great matters, in fact, are won by losing today's game. The issue is to be right, to believe in the right and to pursue it. In truth, Abel was a kind of side victim of Cain's anger with God. We have no idea whether Abel "witnessed" to Cain, or whether he tried to persuade him to righteousness. We only know that when Abel brought his offering to God, he brought it with faith and that Cain killed him precisely because he resented the faith and the character that Abel embodied.

Abel didn't live long, and he didn't "accomplish" anything; but he's a hero of faith. As some people say, "Go figure."

The next great soul in the lexicon of faith heroes is almost equally enigmatic. His name was Enoch. His biography in the book of Genesis is brief but telling. Come to think of it, he is essentially the only person in his particular listing with any biography at all, beyond the barest notice. Enoch appears in a list of names in the fifth chapter of Genesis. The list is stylized: the person is born, lives a stated number of years before having a first son, lives more years with more offspring, and then dies. But not Enoch; he never quite dies, if I may put it that way.

See how Genesis tells his story. Enoch is the son of Jared, and when he was sixty-five he had his first son, Methuselah. Then Enoch's story takes its strange turn: "Enoch walked with God after the birth of Methuselah three hundred years, and had other sons and daughters. Thus all the days of Enoch were three hundred sixty-five years. Enoch walked with God; then he was no more, because God took him" (Genesis 5:22-24). It's a brief story. Its drama is so low-key that a casual reader might easily lose it in the predictable flow of the chapter's obituaries. A careful reader notices that Enoch is different from the rest in that after he has his first child, he walks with God. But then his story becomes as routine as all the others: he has other sons and daughters. Then comes the shocker: he doesn't die like all the rest. The unique quality of his character is repeated—"Enoch walked with God"— and "then he was no more, because God took him."

What is so special about Enoch? He won no wars; we know of no positions that he held. He preached no sermons, nor did he challenge the forces of evil in the manner of Elijah. He just *walked*.

Because I read the sports pages, the term *walked* strikes a chord with me. In college and university football and basketball, promising athletes are awarded scholarships. But there are a limited number of such awards and there's usually room for more players, so schools have young people who are known as "walk-ons." Their athletic skills are not as promising but they love the game and are happy to practice while hoping they may occasionally get to play. Occasionally some of these persons are awarded scholarships later, and now and then one becomes a star. Enoch, so to speak, became a star. He *walked*, and then he *flew*.

Centuries later he appears in the roll call of the faithful in Hebrews 11. Listen: "By faith Enoch was taken so that he did not experience death; and 'he was not found, because God had taken him.' For it was attested before he was taken away that 'he had pleased God'" (Hebrews 11:5).

So how does one "please God"? Our culture measures almost everything by the bottom line of results. But we have no record of results for Enoch—no win-loss record, no accumulated fortune, no evidence of his compelling personality. All he did was *walk*. That, the punster says, is pretty pedestrian. He walked with God, which is of course to walk with very special company, but company available to us all. And from this reference we can infer that Enoch and God got along with each other. You don't choose to have long walks with someone unless you enjoy each other's presence.

The writer of the book of Hebrews rounds out the explanation for us. Having told us that Enoch had faith, he goes on to say that "without faith it is impossible to please God" (Hebrews 11:6). This vigorous sentence doesn't surprise us since this whole chapter of Hebrews is about faith. Nevertheless, it seems pretty dogmatic, especially for those who picture God as being so easy to please that he seems to have no taste whatsoever. God's grace is amazing, no question about that. But God also has some expectations. God expects us to exercise faith.

At this point the ancient apostle does us a huge favor. He adds to his definition of faith: "For whoever would approach [God] must believe that he exists and that he rewards those who seek him" (Hebrews 11:6). This is very helpful. We must believe that

God exists and that God has a certain kind of character, namely, that he notices our attitude and rewards us when it is right. God is not oblivious to the way we think and act. And it appears from the stories of Abel and of Enoch that we are judged not simply by the size of our acts but by the intent and desire of our hearts: that which is behind our words and actions.

To be a person of faith we must believe that God exists! That seems like a minimum admission requirement. How much lower could the bar be set? I think of so many great souls who at first struggled even to believe in God. I think of C. S. Lewis's spiritual journey. First his imagination was baptized, he recalls, then slowly his atheism began to crumble: "That which I greatly feared had at last come upon me." Lewis "admitted that God was God, and knelt and prayed." That night, he writes, he was perhaps "the most dejected and reluctant convert in all England."[3] Lewis had met the minimal requirement, even though he wasn't sure he liked it: he believed that God existed. But that was enough to start with. And if we're to believe the polls, 95 percent or more of the American populace qualifies at this level.

However, the latter half of the requirement is more complicated. It has to do with our opinion of God: what kind of God is God? The kind of God that cares about what goes on in this world? The kind that cares enough, indeed, to be interested even in what people *think* and *believe*? This is unnerving. You see, you and I are inclined to our own kind of con job with God. We go through the motions of religion, sometimes at a pretty minimal level. We attend church, pray at appropriate times, give in a nominal sort of way, and live fairly respectably. But most of us don't really believe that God *rewards those who seek him*. We do, of course, at the times of envy when we wonder why someone else has fared better than we have, or when some supposed misfortune has come and we wonder how God could reward us so poorly.

If we really believed that God rewards those who believe in him, I'm sure we would seek God much more passionately. I suspect that any "reward" we have in mind is very vague or quite insignificant; or still more likely, that what we seek from God is secondary, at best—that is, we seek transient benefits rather than the ultimate good of a deeper relationship with God.

This, clearly, was Enoch's secret. As I have already said, we know nothing of his achievements, his giftedness, or his personality. But this we know: he desired God, so he *walked* with God— nothing glamorous, no report of miracles, just a devotion that made him seek the presence of God daily. The rest is an obituary notice beyond compare.

CHAPTER FIVE

Faith Saves and Condemns

Scripture Reading: Hebrews 11:7

Faith in one form or another is so essential to life that it can be found on every page of human history. Knowingly or not, we humans insist on believing in something. Biblical faith—the kind of faith that interests us in this book and the kind that the writer of Hebrews described—has its seasons. Henry Van Dyke, the preacher, poet, and statesman, classified the late nineteenth century as an "age of doubt"; some historians have christened the Middle Ages as the "age of faith." Presumably it is easier to believe—or to doubt—in some periods than in others.

This seems altogether logical. In fact, it's probably so logical that usually we don't give the matter much attention. The spirit of the times in which we live is so familiar—perhaps even comfortable—that we take it for granted, like the air we breathe. At a later time, social or intellectual historians, with the advantage of perspective, classify our times for us.

It's easy to identify the faith quality of the times in which Noah lived. They were bad times—very bad. The biblical writer gives us the impression that they were about as bad as they could get. Listen: "The LORD saw that the wickedness of humankind was great in the earth, and that every inclination of the thoughts of their hearts was only evil continually" (Genesis 6:5). No wonder, then, that "the earth was filled with violence" (Genesis 6:11); if the only thought in the mind is evil, there is nothing to restrain violence. The times were so bad that "the LORD was sorry that he had made humankind on the earth, and it grieved him to his heart" (Genesis 6:6).

I can't enlarge much on this. I have lived through a variety of changes in my rather long lifetime—through classic economic depression, the Second World War, and ensuing political and social changes. I have seen conduct that was once decried become conduct glorified, and violence that would once have been discussed in hushed tones become commonplace in family-room entertainment; but I've never seen a world where "every inclination of the thoughts of their hearts was only evil continually." We aren't as easily shocked as were some other generations, but the thoughts of our hearts are more often good—or at least passive—than evil.

It's hard for us to imagine the degree of evil in Noah's time. It was a world where you weren't safe on the streets by day or by night. We have neighborhoods like that in our world; but in Noah's story the whole world was like that. And in Noah's world it did no good to step into what should be the security of home, because you couldn't be sure of loyalty within your own family. There was no place to hide.

So how do you manage in such a world? The general idea is to outevil evil. That's the idea behind the words "every inclination of the thoughts of their hearts was only evil continually." In a culture where intelligence is prized, you try to be smarter than the average; in a world of athletic prowess, you try to break the records; in a world where evil is the measure, you seek to set a new standard for what is the worst.

In such a world, the thought of God ceases to exist. In evil times we lose confidence in other people, then in ourselves, then in the very principles of right and wrong, and finally, in God. We come to feel—at first subtly, then boldly—that if so much evil exists and nothing is done about it, one of two conclusions is inevitable: either there is no God—no goodness—or if there is, then this is a God who doesn't care. And if God doesn't care, why should we?

Such was the world in which Noah lived. The presence of evil was so constant that there was no room for good, no place where goodness or purity or hope could take a tiny foothold. And at that time, in those circumstances, "Noah was a righteous man, blameless in his generation." How can you be blameless in a time when all the evaluations are tilted utterly to evil? How do you keep your moorings when there is no compass pointing north? It would be enough to drive a soul mad. But Noah somehow believed. Like Enoch centuries earlier, he "walked with God" (Genesis 6:9). But whereas Enoch was singularly taken from the scene, Noah was thrust into his times with an intensity that made him utterly contrary to all that was around him.

Noah's story is one of those anomalies of human history. It is the story of goodness so great that it not only survives in the midst of evil, it thrives there. The evil that makes others acquiesce makes the Noah-type more obstinately good. This story has been lived out in one form or another at every level from periods of world history to individual households. At a time in nineteenth-century England when even the most earnest Christians saw certain areas of London as places to bequeath to hell, William and Catherine Booth saw them as places to crusade for Christ. The result was the Salvation Army. When brutality was glorified in the Roman coliseum and the taking of human life was entertainment, one astonishing soul turned the tide. As a pastor I have seen character burst forth with beauty in households where every prevailing force was cheap and ugly. How can this happen? Call it the Noah miracle, the survival of goodness against all the massive, apparently unchangeable putridness of evil.

So the times were bad, perhaps impossibly bad. But there was Noah—a righteous man in the midst of all this evil, a flower in the rubbish of approved and acclaimed degradation. He was a person of faith. And faith is never more at home than in the back side of life. Hear me: you hardly know what faith is like, what its potential is, how charming its laughter, until you see faith in a world where it is so odd, so apparently out of place.

The story that follows is fascinating. I ask you to read it for its message. Don't get lost in the incidentals of weather forecasting, animal husbandry, naval architecture, and carpentry. God told Noah how greatly disappointed he was in the conduct of the human race and said that the only solution was to wipe out the sorry mess and make a new start.

Then God told Noah to make a great boat, roughly 450 feet long, 75 feet wide, and 45 feet high, with three decks, and to take on the boat the eight members of his own family, representatives of the animal kingdom, and plenty of food. The Bible says, "Noah did this; he did all that God commanded him" (Genesis 6:22). That sentence is the measure of Noah's faith. Noah's faith is measured at a carpenter's bench with boards and tools and is announced with the beat of a hammer.

I'm sure Noah's neighbors always thought he was a little odd. In a society where filth, violence, and deception were the rule, Noah was righteous, kindly, and honest. Of course his neighbors thought him odd. So when he began building this architectural monstrosity in his field, they judged he had now slipped over the edge. For a time, surely Noah's neighbors mocked him; then, almost surely, they came to ignore him. I think this is what is implied in Jesus' words when he said that in the days of Noah the people "were eating and drinking, marrying and giving in marriage, . . . and they knew nothing until the flood came and swept them all away" (Matthew 24:38-39). The people got used to Noah and his preachments, and they went on with life as usual.

One of faith's greatest tests is when the faith-advocate is simply ignored. Faith has an easier time with outright opposition than with condescending acceptance. When people oppose you, you know they're taking you seriously; but when they ignore you, you cease to be an issue. Faith has to learn to survive inattention as well as opposition.

At last Noah finished building his ark, and still nothing had happened. Not one hopeful cloud, so to speak, had appeared in the sky. Life was going on in its usual way; folk were "eating and drinking, marrying and giving in marriage." What could be more normal? I'm judging by my own personality, but I'm almost certain that sometimes Noah looked out at his project and wondered why God had ever told him to build. Yes, and more than that: he must sometimes have wondered if it was really God who spoke to him. Perhaps his neighbors were right; perhaps he was a bit over the edge. You don't have to be a fanatic to be good, do you? Wasn't it enough that he was honest and kind? Why this ark-building business? Did Noah sometimes have such thoughts as he fell asleep in tears of confusion and frustration?

I'm just trying to say that I can't believe Noah lived all those years in perfect equanimity. Noah was a man of faith, no doubt about that, but this doesn't mean that he was never pursued by doubt. Faith shows its integrity not in its never doubting, but in rising above its doubts and in continuing on its journey.

As I see it, Noah's more trying day is still ahead. The writer of Genesis says nothing about it, but I see it in the way the writer of Hebrews summarizes his evaluation of Noah's faith. One day God tells Noah to load the ark; in seven days the rains will come. But it was more than rain. As the Scriptures tell it, "All the fountains of the great deep burst forth, and the windows of the heavens were opened" (Genesis 7:11). Water came from above and below. It is as if the separation of "waters from the waters" at the time of creation (Genesis 1:6-8) was temporarily abrogated.

Here is the dark chapter for Noah. He is the deliverer of a remnant, the one who provides the new start, but thus he is also the one who presides over the judgment of destruction. The New Testament puts it this way: "By faith Noah, warned by God about events as yet unseen, respected the warning and built an ark to save his household; by this he condemned the world and became an heir to the righteousness that is in accordance with faith" (Hebrews 11:7).

Here is more of the back side of faith. Faith not only delivers; it condemns. By his faith, Noah *condemned the world.* Does this mean there would have been no flood if it were not for Noah? No; rather there would have been no survivors if it were not for Noah. The judgments of life fall whether there is a Noah or not. When Noah's faith guarantees the future he also condemns those who do not have faith, because he proves that a different kind of life is possible. In Noah's world, where all thought and all conduct were set on evil, one could conclude that it was impossible for anyone to be good, that the tide of evil was simply too powerful to be countered. But by faith Noah proved otherwise. Thus Noah's faith and the life that ensued from it condemned the world.

People of faith bless us, but they also force us to deal with our supposed limitations. I remember when the athletic world considered a four-minute mile unattainable. As long as that was the belief, a champion distance runner could be comfortable with a 4:10 mile. But once a runner broke the four-minute barrier, all other distance runners came under judgment. When the impossible is no longer impossible, we are left without excuse.

That's why truly fine people, people of faith, make some of us uncomfortable. We admire their achievements if they are fairly well removed from us, either in time or in style of life, but they upset us if they belong to our times and our way of living. William Barclay reminds us that one of the finest men in ancient Athens was Aristides. He was so fine that they called him "Aristides the just." Eventually, however, they voted to banish and to ostracize him. One man, when asked why he had so voted, answered, "Because I am tired of hearing Aristides called 'the just.' "[1] Achieving people make us nervous—especially virtuous achieving people. It wasn't surprising that people began looking for shortcomings in Mother Teresa in the latter years of her work— shameful, but not surprising. Excellence condemns us because it means that possibly, just possibly, we could be better than we are. So instead of learning the secrets of excellence we try to diminish its attractiveness. Lord, help us!

Thank God there is also something in us that wants to be like Noah. We long for the faith to stand against the tide of our times, to believe in the impossible dream, to commit to God and to goodness no matter what the contemporary culture dictates. We think of John Brown in the days of American slavery. It was generally believed that slavery was essential to the American economy. It was written into the Constitution in the three-fifths rule; some argued it was justified in the Bible. Many hated slavery, but it seemed invincible. John Brown believed it was so wrong that, against all odds, he fought it. I doubt that he fought it wisely, and he was hanged for treason. But when the Union troops marched as the Civil War began, they sang, "John Brown's body lies a-moldering in the grave, / His soul goes marching on." His faith helped turn the tide.

Every Noah makes us nervous because Noah-type faith condemns us. We know—all of us know—that we shouldn't acquiesce to the evils of our time. There is a seed of faith in every soul that makes us uncomfortable with evil, with shoddy living, and with spiritual mediocrity. And often, just when we are growing comfortable with the kind of status quo that ought to upset us, some Noah comes along to remind us that things ought not to be this way.

I should warn you (and warn myself) that not every Noah wins—not in his or her lifetime or his or her setting. Between the lines in the history books are names we've never heard, great souls who believed and who struggled but who apparently lost. But faith doesn't have to win this election, this scholarship, or this battle. Faith believes so passionately in goodness, mercy, and truth that it can lose today and still march with head held high tomorrow. The tears of its defeats are swallowed up by the laughter of its anticipation.

I believe that God is constantly on the watch for the Noah-type soul, because there are always settings where evil is so dominant that it is only a matter of time until some flood will destroy. Believe me, wherever there is evil there is eventually some flood because there is built into evil its own seeds of judgment. So God keeps looking for the Noah-type souls.

Sometimes those souls operate on the broad canvas of history where later generations revere them for what they did. Other Noah-type souls function in a few square blocks in some neighborhood of addiction and gang warfare where their lives are cut short by an errant bullet and they're remembered only by some sibling or cousin who resolves, because of them, to do better. Or perhaps they're remembered only by God; I cannot say which. Some find their place only in their financial support of a cherished cause or on those occasions when they speak a contending word when the discussion loses all respect for purity and truth and where someone's reputation is maligned and no one rises in defense. I believe God is always looking for the Noah-type soul: faith when all is against it.

People often asked Jesus how to be prepared for the kingdom of God and for his return. One day Jesus answered by using a reference to the days of Noah and of Lot, and then he told a parable about the importance of prayer, the kind of prayer that never gives up. He finished the story with a question: "When the Son of Man comes, will he find faith on earth?" (Luke 17:20–18:8). That is, will he find faith of the Noah-type soul? It is a faith that holds on when all is against it, a faith that condemns us by reminding us that faith matters, win or lose, because it is right.

CHAPTER SIX

Faith Is a Family Affair

Scripture Reading: Hebrews 11:8-13

Faith is a hardy virtue, yet it's difficult to pass from one generation to another. It seems easily to lose its distinctive features along the way. I remember the university history professor who spoke with amusement of the fortunes the children of missionaries made in Hawaii. "Christian missionaries went to Hawaii to do good," he said, "and their children stayed there to do well." And I recall the painful spiritual history summarized by an anonymous Englishman. "My father marched the streets of England for Christ," he said. "I marched for great causes. My children aren't marching for anything."

The truth is that faith has to be born anew in every generation. If it isn't you may see a slight family resemblance from one generation to the next but the distinctive reality will be gone. The crucial secret is for each generation to realize that it is their primary business to make their faith a living, appealing thing to their families and to the generation that follows. It seems that this should be easy: faith is such a grand, sustaining, achieving virtue that surely every generation would want it. But of course faith also comes with a price, a sell-everything-to-get-it kind of price, so other family members have to be willing to pay the price. Besides, faith is intangible, which always makes it a hard sell until people sense its reality.

Let me tell you about some people who made faith a family affair. Their names have an iconic rhythm in the Bible, a rhythm that persists to our own day. One might almost call it the rhythm of faith: Abraham, Isaac, and Jacob.

The story begins with Abraham—or *Abram*, as he was known when the story opens. He lived in the ancient city of Ur, one of the great cities of his time. It appears that he belonged to an achieving family, one led by a rather adventuresome father, Terah, who led the family out of Ur with the intention of moving to Canaan. They stopped, however, in the city of Haran, where Terah died. There Abraham settled until one day God spoke to him, telling him to uproot his life and go. No destination was given. He was told just to go.

It was to be a fierce uprooting. "Go from your country and your kindred and your father's house" (Genesis 12:1). Those few words are a summary of what most of us hold dear. "Your country": one's country is dear; even people who have fled from a tyrannical government often say that they never stop loving the soil of their homeland. "Your kindred": family ties are often a mixed blessing, but it's a rare person who wants to sever such ties completely. "Your father's house": all those intimacies, memories and comfortable culture patterns—those intangibles that make life beautiful. How does one leave them all?

And leave them for what? "The land that I will show you" (Genesis 12:1). God is calling Abraham to give up all that he knows for something he doesn't know, to forsake the certain for the uncertain. To be honest, God sounds a little like the salesman or financial counselor who says, "Just trust me." And remember, as far as we know, Abraham was happy in Haran. It isn't as if poverty, failed crops, or a murderous regime drove him out. Indeed, the call makes clear that Abraham is being asked to give up the very things most of us want to hold on to.

As I see it, it is at this point that faith first becomes a family affair. The biblical writer refers to Abraham's wife a few verses earlier, mentioning her by name (Sarai; later to be known as Sarah) three times in three verses (Genesis 11:29-31). The writer even tells us that "Sarai was barren; she had no child" (Genesis 11:30). All of this indicates that Sarah was no nonentity. Later in the story we'll see what a strong and in fact willful woman she was. I can't imagine her making this life-altering move at this time in her life without voicing her opinion.

But she went. Abraham went because he had faith in God. Sarah went because she had faith in Abraham and in Abraham's testimony about God.

I have profound regard for the Sarah type of faith. I have seen it any number of times in the parents of missionaries. "Our son and daughter-in-law feel God has called them to Africa. We hated like anything to see them go; but they feel it's God's will." In a sense, this is secondhand faith, but I believe it has firsthand quality. I remember the husband of a seminary student. "My wife sensed that she had a call, so I quit my job and we moved here so

she could go to seminary." At a secular level I think of a manu-
facturer and his wife who told me of their early days and of the
wife's belief in her husband's future. "Every night after work," he
said, "I developed my product in our garage. Clara packaged it for
mailing, kept the financial records, and did the correspondence."
Yes, I believe in the Sarah type of faith: secondhand faith with
firsthand quality.

This kind of family faith operates every day in all of the great
causes that matter. My only call to Thailand, Benin, Ghana,
Kenya, and several other countries is in our Lord's general call to
"go into all the world," but I give financial support to the work of
Christ in those places because I believe in the call of my former stu-
dents who are serving there. It is the same kind of secondhand faith
that has inspired our family to support a seminary, a Christian university, and homes for children and youth and for the aging. It is a
Sarah-type faith—a faith in the person who has the call and that
sees it as a privilege to be part of that person's call.

When God called Abraham it was with the promise that he
and Sarah would have a son. They waited a very long while
before the promise was fulfilled, and in the meanwhile the faith
of both Abraham and Sarah wavered more than once. At times
it wavered so perilously that it looked as if the purposes of God
might be waylaid. But in time their faith was rewarded and in
time they had a son named Isaac. The name was appropriate:
laughter. I think the name reflects the laughter both of their faith
and of their unbelief. We can employ laughter both ways, you
know—in hope and in derision. But in mercy, God accepts our
mixed laughter, because our faith is only rarely a pure faith. Most

of the time our faith can be measured by degrees of purity and by the varying forms of its laughter.

We don't know how Abraham communicated his faith to his son Isaac. We know, however, that he was commissioned to do so. Roughly a year before Isaac was born God told Abraham, "As for you, you shall keep my covenant, you and your offspring after you throughout their generations" (Genesis 17:9), at which point Abraham was given the signature to the covenant, the rite of circumcision. By its very nature the rite reflected the idea of generational fruitfulness as if to say that the power of procreation was also marked by the fact of the covenant with God. To have a child meant to have a responsibility to raise that child within the covenant.

Abraham knew that his relationship with God was meant to be passed on. God's business with him was not to end with him; it was something for his offspring "throughout their generations." It would have been unthinkable for Abraham to have said, as twenty-first-century parents sometimes do, "My children's faith is their own business; let them decide when the time comes." Abraham's power to procreate was an obligation to continue the faith; the obligation was written into the nature of the covenant, circumcision.

Every person's faith is singularly his or her own, but the possessors of faith in any generation are responsible to do everything in their power to communicate that faith to the next generation. We think it is monstrous when we read that a parent has abandoned a child to starvation. I submit that it is still more monstrous for a parent to abandon a child to spiritual starvation. If it is evil (as surely it is!) for a parent to be unconcerned or uncaring about the physical life of a child, what shall we say of a parent who neglects a child's eternal nourishment and welfare?

I try to imagine how Abraham conveyed faith to Isaac. Did he tell Isaac how God had called him when he and Sarah still lived in Haran, or how the first step toward Canaan, the land of promise, began with Isaac's grandfather, Terah? I can't help feeling that he did, because these experiences were too seminal in his life to be left unspoken to his son. Blessed is the family that tells children that they participate in generations of faith! I'm also confident that Abraham lived out the character of his faith in the conduct of farm, of family, and of daily business and human relationships.

The single instance in which Abraham conveyed faith most forcefully to Isaac is in the incident we will examine in the next chapter, but let me touch on it here. When Isaac was entering young manhood, at a point where his potential was obvious and with it his capacity to carry on the covenant between God and Abraham, God issued a strange, apparently irrational command to Abraham: "Take your son, your only son Isaac, whom you love, and go to the land of Moriah, and offer him there as a burnt offering on one of the mountains that I shall show you" (Genesis 22:2).

When the command says "your only son Isaac," it puts the covenant in controversy with itself. Isaac was the key element in the covenant. If Abraham were to become—as promised—the father of "a great nation," he had to have offspring. Earlier when Abraham suggested to God that Ishmael might be the one, God insisted that the child was to be a product of the union of Abraham and Sarah. So now God identifies Isaac as "your only son"—the one, indeed, through whom the covenant is fulfilled.

The three-day walk to the mountain of sacrifice is somber enough, but when Abraham and Isaac leave the two young servants who had accompanied them, Isaac asks a to-the-point question: "The fire and the wood are here, but where is the lamb for a burnt offering?" Abraham answers simply and succinctly, "God himself will provide the lamb for a burnt offering, my son" (Genesis 22:7-8). Not long after, Isaac is tied and laid on the altar on top of the wood, and the knife is raised to kill him. However, God intervenes and a ram, "caught in a thicket by its horns," is sacrificed instead (22:13).

At no point in this dramatic incident are we given any insight into Isaac's thoughts, nor is there any record of a catechetical lesson from Abraham to his son. But if ever an object lesson was passed from a parent to a child, here is one. Bible scholars, novelists, poets, and playwrights have examined this scene. Some feel that Isaac was estranged from his father after this time; thus when we read the story of Isaac's marriage to Rebekah, we're told that Isaac "brought her into his mother Sarah's tent" and that "he loved her" and "was comforted after his mother's death" (Genesis 24:67)—all of it suggesting that Isaac's mother, Sarah, had been his emotional support. Those who suggest that the sacrifice experience put a barrier between Isaac and his father also note that Genesis records no further conversation between the father and son after this incident.

All such conjecturing is good material for a novelist or, for that matter, a preacher. It cannot be proved or disproved. I submit, in any event, that the long walk from home to the land of Moriah was a faith walk for Isaac as well as for Abraham and that the faith of Abraham was communicated to his son through this iconic incident. Isaac saw that his father believed in the God of the covenant even more than in the miracle—Isaac, himself—that was the fulfillment of the covenant and that his father believed that God would not abandon the covenant, no matter what human circumstances might indicate. He saw, too, that God did, in fact, provide a sacrifice. Abraham taught faith to Isaac, no doubt about it. It was no conventional classroom, but the teacher, the student, and the lesson were all present.

We have no record of Isaac's spiritual influence on his son Jacob. The writer of Genesis makes clear that Isaac preferred the company of his older son, Esau, to that of Jacob, and that "Rebekah loved Jacob," who was a quiet man and a homebody (Genesis 25:27-28). Further, God had revealed to Rebekah during her pregnancy that the elder of her twins would serve the younger (Genesis 25:23). I have a feeling that Rebekah played the major part in teaching Jacob about the family covenant—and particularly, his place in that covenant. It is hardly the last time that a mother became a family's primary caretaker of the faith covenant. Rebekah no doubt stepped out of bounds in urging and empowering Jacob to deceive his father in order to get the elder son's blessing, but I urge us to respect her intentions even while we reject the way she deployed them.

The point that stands out for the writer of our faith essay in the Letter to Hebrews is this: Isaac and Jacob, Abraham's son and grandson, carried on the faith journey that Abraham had started. They too embraced a nomadic life, "as in a foreign land, living in tents," even though it was the land that "had been promised" to them; they too "were heirs with [Abraham] of the same promise" (Hebrews 11:9). And particularly, Isaac and Jacob clung to the vision that Abraham had first embraced when "he looked forward to the city that has foundations, whose architect and builder is God" (Hebrews 11:10).

I must note at least in passing the back-side quality of faith that energized these three men and the women who invested their lives with them. They had a vision, a grand vision, of "the city that has foundations, whose architect and builder is God," and because that vision was so dominant in their souls, they were content to live in *tents*. These tents were not poverty structures. I remember celebrating New Year's Eve in a tent outside Cairo, Egypt, some years ago. Its floors had oriental carpets, and I suspect that the tents of Abraham, Isaac, and Jacob were also comfortable and well appointed in ways that are hard for our house and apartment dwellers to imagine. But the crucial issue is this: they had a temporary quality. Still more significant is that, temporary or not, these three men, their spouses, and their children lived out their lives—their *faith* lives—in such dwellings. They never got to settle in brick and mortar—all because they had a vision of a city with *foundations*: God's city.

They never got to see this city, except by faith. They lived in tents, on a journey—all three of them knowing what Abraham knew, that he went "not knowing where he was going" (Hebrews 11:8). Poor directional system! But they kept going, with a sublime confidence in their destination. This was a family faith. Abraham passed it to Isaac, and Isaac (perhaps primarily with Rebekah's help) passed it to Jacob.

Let me interrupt our visit here with a kind of spiritual sidebar. This biblical story is about the conveying of faith through a blood family. But a word should also be spoken about faith families that exist entirely at a spiritual level, without the benefit of any physical family tree. You may trace your faith covenant to such a spiritual lineage, entirely or partly. I am grateful that both heritages have operated in my life. My parents were earnest Christians, impressive in their desire to pass their faith along to their children. I owe a major, primary debt to them and to the week-by-week loyalty with which they supported their faith.

But I am almost equally grateful to a long list of Sunday school teachers, pastors and evangelists, and the people who bothered to greet me after church, often to express their interest in the state of my soul. It would be easy for me to make a list to compare with the opening chapters of 1 Chronicles if I thought you would take the time to read it. I want only to say, with unapologetic emotion, that these people too are my kin, my spiritual family. They are persons who passed on the faith to me.

Faith is a family affair. At best it is passed through our physical family, the people with whom we live and whose bloodstream we share. But just as surely it is passed through the people who enter our lives by their faith commitments and from whom we gain or sustain our own walk of faith. The obligation then, for you and for me, is to pass along this hardy but strangely delicate gift—our faith—so that someday someone will list us as one of his or her faith ancestors.

CHAPTER SEVEN

Faith Takes a Test

Scripture Reading: Hebrews 11:17-19

We are about to visit one of the most important and most difficult stories in the Bible. Some people wish this incident had never happened or that it had never been recorded and made part of the biblical story. The story makes many readers uneasy, and it makes others angry. Not only does the story appear in the Old Testament book of Genesis, but also the writer of the New Testament book of Hebrews includes it in the record of the great faith events, the events that are intended to inspire our living. It's obvious that the New Testament writer isn't uneasy about the story and that he certainly isn't embarrassed by it. He embraces the story as his own and wants us to do the same.

This probably indicates that other generations were more tough-minded about life than we are. Indeed, we might find that our contemporaries outside of Europe and North America read this story differently than we do. And if we think that this is because these persons are less educated than we are, we need to remind ourselves that one of the most sophisticated thinkers of nineteenth-century Europe, Søren Kierkegaard, was not troubled by this story as some in our generation are. Kierkegaard was moved by the story but he refused to treat it superficially or to try to explain it away. The story is in the Scriptures of the Old and New Testament for good reason. We do well, therefore, to see why this story has been recorded in the Old Testament and made exemplary in the New, and what it can mean to us in our twenty-first-century faith journey.

Above all, of course, this story is a faith story, and in its unique way it shows faith from the back side—or perhaps I should say from an angle we'd rather not deal with.

I am referring to that strange, mystical, upsetting record in the twenty-second chapter of Genesis. The opening sentence is a warning signal: "After these things God tested Abraham" (Genesis 22:1). After what "things"? It was after Abraham had been through a series of trying, contentious situations, first within his own family, in being forced to send away Hagar and Ishmael, and then in some business relations with Abimelech, the ruler of the area—an incident that concludes, "And Abraham resided as an alien many days in the land of the Philistines" (Genesis 21:34). Abraham, who had left his homeland to follow God's bidding, is still an alien. This was a time when Abraham badly needed some reassurance from God. Instead, God tested him. It's as if the family and business problems were only warm-up games before the big tournament began.

God gave Abraham an outrageous order. After a long generation of Abraham's faith journey, at a time when it seemed Abraham's faith was now entering the phase of fulfillment and reward, a kind of faith-retirement era, God "tested" him. And the test was as if a spiritual archer had aimed his arrow at the heart-center of Abraham's very being. "Take your son, your only son Isaac, whom you love, and go to the land of Moriah, and offer him there as a burnt offering on one of the mountains that I shall show you" (Genesis 22:2). The specific elements in this call are painful. Who is this son who is to be sacrificed? "Your only son Isaac [the one who makes you laugh], whom you love." Some might say God is being spiteful in enunciating the issue so clearly. I think, rather, that God is making clear that he knows what he is asking Abraham and that he knows what is going on in Abraham's soul when he receives the call.

The ultimate nature of the sacrifice is also clear. It is not only that Isaac is to be killed, but also that he is to become "a burnt offering": the kind of offering, that is, that leaves only ashes. I think, too, that Abraham catches a reminiscent note in a detail of this command. The event is to happen "on one of the mountains that I shall show you." This sounds like a reprise of Abraham's original call, many years before, when God told him to leave all to go "to the land that I will show you" (Genesis 12:1). After years of faithfulness, here is God's reward to Abraham: once again he is to walk by faith, with no road map, no named destination. One thinks that by now God will treat this great faith-soul as a confidant, telling him some of the details of the journey. Instead, God handles him like a foot soldier. Just when you might think your faith has brought you some rights, you discover you're back at the recruiting station.

So how does Abraham respond? Just as he did decades earlier. We're not told of his inner struggle, which must surely have existed. We are told only this: "So Abraham rose early in the morning [and] saddled his donkey" (Genesis 22:3). It is as matter of fact as if Abraham were preparing for a morning trip to the market.

As I see it, however, this trip was even more momentous than that one many years before when Abraham and Sarah and their whole economic enterprise left Haran for the unknown. On that day, they left home and family—that is, they left the past. This time Abraham—in sacrificing Isaac—was leaving the future. That time, Abraham took a whole retinue of employees. This time, he took two of the young men from his establishment. That time, Sarah accompanied Abraham. This time, Abraham is alone. Did Abraham leave Sarah behind out of respect for her health and her maternal sensibilities? Perhaps. Or did Sarah refuse to go on such a trip? Or did Abraham keep the purpose of the trip a secret from his wife? We can only speculate. All we know is that Sarah was not part of the lonely journey. I'm sure it was all the lonelier because she wasn't there. They had traveled together for a long lifetime, but this was to be a solitary journey for Abraham—and a solitary Sarah at home.

I note that Abraham "cut the wood for the burnt offering" (Genesis 22:3), just as earlier he had saddled his donkey. I understand why he saddled his donkey; often a rider feels close enough to his animal that he likes to take care of such a detail for himself. But why did Abraham cut the wood? This was work for his servants, and goodness knows he had a full retinue. Was it the restlessness of a person who has to keep occupied in order to keep his mind off the day that lies ahead? Or was it something in Abraham that saw the sacrifice wood as something so sacred that he must himself prepare it?

So they walked. For the better part of three days they walked. They walked long enough for Abraham to change his mind or to ask questions of God; long enough for Abraham to suggest to God that he be allowed to die in Isaac's place. As a father, I wonder if Abraham made such a counteroffer to God. Then, on the third day, "Abraham looked up and saw the place far away" (Genesis 22:4). Abraham had set out on this journey knowing only that it would end at "one of the mountains" that God would show him. Somehow he knew now that this was the mountain. So he told the two young men, "Stay here with the donkey; the boy and I will go over there; we will worship, and then we will come back to you" (Genesis 22:5).

Since the donkey was being left behind, Abraham now "took the wood of the burnt offering and laid it on his son Isaac" (Genesis 22:6). A Christian reading this story thinks of Jesus carrying his own cross until he is crushed by the load and the cross is given to a passerby, Simon of Cyrene. In any event, I'm sure the writer of Genesis wants us to see the irony in Isaac's having to carry the wood on which he will be sacrificed while Abraham carries the knife and the fire. "So the two of them walked on together" (Genesis 22:6). Then Isaac asks a question, a question as practical as the sort people ask on any journey, a question having to do with provisions for the trip: "The fire and the wood are here, but where is the lamb for a burnt offering?" (Genesis 22:7).

Abraham replies, "God himself will provide the lamb for a burnt offering, my son" (Genesis 22:8).

What shall we say of Abraham's answer? It wouldn't work in most contemporary American families; the boy would have a series of follow-up questions. But the world of Abraham and Isaac was one where a father's answer was complete and allowing of no further inquiry no matter how brief or unsatisfactory it might seem to be. And of course, it was a faith answer, and I am confident that because of earlier faith discussions, Isaac was satisfied with his father's succinct statement.

Abraham had lived with faith issues for more than a quarter of a century, ever since God commissioned him at Haran, and though the faith issues had many intricate parts, Isaac was the linchpin that held everything else together. Abraham had left all of the certainties of life in Haran to seek out a new world and a new way of life. However, the promise that gave content to the new world was the promise that he and Sarah would have a son so that through them all the families of the earth would be blessed. They waited twenty-five years for that son, God rejecting any lesser solution. Now the son was to be taken from them— by order of the God who had promised the son and whose miracle had brought the son to birth.

That previous paragraph may seem a cold, religious handling of a feverish human experience. Believe me, the father in me has all the other feelings as well. I remember when my daughter was only three, an age when she still settled into my lap every evening to be read to from *Childcraft* and *Winnie the Pooh*, when an earlier mistaken diagnosis led to an emergency appendectomy on a Saturday evening. When I read Isaac's question about the lamb, I hear my daughter pleading as I carried her into the hospital, "Don't let them hurt me, Daddy." And I remember the morning, three days after the surgery, when the doctor rose to his full height after examining her and said, "She's going to live." So I read the story from Moriah at two levels—as a father who knows parental feelings, and as someone who just now is trying to lead us in a study of faith.

I'm sure Abraham's experience operated at both levels. He was a parent who was also a man of faith. When God sent him on this three-day journey of sacrifice, it was with the words "your only son Isaac, *whom you love*," as if to say, "I know what I'm asking you to do." However, at this point we're looking at Abraham as a human being who was on a faith journey, and we are examining that journey's eternal dimensions: the faith of a man who has bet his life on what he perceives to be the plan of God and who now sees the essential feature in the plan, Isaac, about to be removed—worse, removed by his own hand and by God's order.

The person who gave us the faith hall of fame in the book of Hebrews insists on our seeing the spiritual implications of the whole matter, so much so that he says nothing about the human side of a loving father. The New Testament writer tells us that this man "who had received the promises was ready to offer up his only son, of whom he had been told, 'It is through Isaac that descendants shall be named for you'" (Hebrews 11:17-18). He wants us to understand that when God called for the sacrificing of Isaac he seemed to be contradicting the promise he had made when Abraham was called, and the promise that was reaffirmed on several succeeding occasions. God seemed, that is, to be in conflict with God's own self.

The Genesis story itself hints strongly about the faith with which Abraham proceeded on his dramatic three-day trip to Moriah. You remember that when Abraham and Isaac left the two young servants Abraham explained that they were going farther for their worship. And then he gave his faith declaration: "We will worship, and then we will come back to you" (Genesis 22:5). *"We will come back to you."* Abraham is utterly confident that whatever happens on that mountain, he and Isaac will return. I think it is this sentence that the writer of Hebrews 11 has in mind centuries later when he writes his commentary on the incident. He says of Abraham, "He considered the fact that God is able even to raise someone from the dead—and figuratively speaking, he did receive him back" (Hebrews 11:19).

That is, Abraham accepted the death of Isaac as a fact. He proceeded on that epochal walk expecting that Isaac would die—but with the sublime certainty that God would see to it that Isaac would live again. Abraham had not forgotten a time many years earlier, before Isaac was born, when he had suggested to God, "O that Ishmael might live in your sight"—that is, that Ishmael, son of the handmaiden Hagar, might be the recipient of God's favor and be the one through whom Abraham would bless the ages— and God had answered, "No, but your wife Sarah shall bear you a son, and you shall name him Isaac" (Genesis 17:18-19).

Whatever might happen on that mountain—that mountain where only Abraham, Isaac, and God would be present, where not even the donkey would stand as a witness—Isaac would live.

No matter if Isaac's blood was shed; no matter if his strapping young body was reduced to ashes; Isaac would come down the mountain with him. Abraham knew it. He knew it because he believed in the character of God and because he was certain beyond circumstances and contradiction and all signs to the contrary that God, who had covenanted with him, would be true to the promise.

This story is sacred ground. I have wondered if Jesus pondered it as he prayed in Gethsemane that if possible the cup of suffering be taken from him, but if not, that the Father's will would be done. And did he think of Isaac carrying the bundle of wood at Moriah as he himself began carrying the cross to Golgotha? And when Jesus cried, "My God, why have you forsaken me?" (Mark 15:34), did he remember Isaac while knowing that he himself would have to go to the place of the dead until the third day? Perhaps he did.

I confess that I don't like the way this story begins: "After these things God tested Abraham" (Genesis 22:1). I don't like the idea of God "testing" people. But this much I know, and so do you if you have lived long enough to read this story: life has its testing places. Whatever the source of our tests, we have them. Tests are an integral, inescapable part of being human. Sir William Osler, whose medical genius towered first in Canada, then in the United States, and at last in Great Britain, said, "Nothing in life is more wonderful than faith—the one great moving force which we can neither weigh in the balance nor test in the crucible."[1]

But of course there is a crucible where faith is tested. It's called *life*. Blessed are those who pass the test.

CHAPTER EIGHT

Faith Can Be Communicated

Scripture Reading: Hebrews 11:20-23

When I was a young minister I wondered why human moral progress couldn't move on as surely and predictably as its physical progress. Biology, physics, mathematics, chemistry—in all of these the new generation builds upon the achievements of the previous one. "There's no need to reinvent the wheel," as the saying goes, and physical progress lives by that axiom.

But not so with moral progress. We humans have known for thousands of years that love is better than hate, peace is better than war, truth is better than deception—even something so objective as efficiency is better than disorder—and yet we insist on relearning these matters generation after generation. I can promise you that if there is a *New York Times* list of best-selling books ten or twenty years from now, the list will include "new secrets" for happiness, love, success, contentment, and fulfillment, and that when you read those "new secrets" you will discover that they're saying what humans have known and said for as far back as we know.

Deep down, we know why: because every generation is Adam and Eve. Every generation—no, more precisely, every human being—insists on finding out for itself what is true and beautiful and honorable and fulfilling. And so it is with that extraordinary power that God has entrusted to us humans, faith.

Here's the good news: all of these moral qualities—including faith—can be communicated from one generation to another. Here's the bad news: so can the qualities of immorality and destruction, including unfaith, or unbelief, or faith in the wrong ideas and principles.

But wait; there's still more good news. God is on the side of faith and truth and love and justice. God has an eternal stake in this long struggle between right and wrong. Therefore, you and I can enter the ramparts for faith with the grand confidence that God is on our side, enlightening and empowering us for victory. We can be assured of God's help as we seek to communicate faith to others in our own generation and to the generation next to come.

In fact, if there is to be faith in this generation, or the next, or until God's millennium, it will be present because of those persons who are among us just now. This is the generation of the faithful. The very fact that I'm writing this book and that you're reading it is *prima facie* evidence of that. Perhaps this strikes you as rather modest evidence, so I should hasten to say that it's only one piece in a maze of matters; but it is one, and it's right here in our hands.

The whole idea of such communication goes back to the early days of the Bible record of faith, as I have already indicated. I spoke earlier about faith being a family affair, passing from Abraham to Isaac and from Isaac to Jacob—father to son to grandson. The New Testament writer makes this progression very clear: "By faith Isaac invoked blessings *for the future* on Jacob and Esau" (Hebrews 11:20; italics mine). Isaac—a kind of quiet interlude between his father, Abraham, and his son, Jacob—nevertheless is specifically identified for his eye "for the future."

It's interesting, too, that he saw the future for both his sons, not simply the one through whom the "promise" was to travel; because while God works in special ways through special people, God is also at work throughout our human race. Indeed, at times God seems to specialize in going outside the ordained circle to accomplish the eternal purposes, as we shall note just a little later. The primary work is through Jacob, but faith is also operating through Esau—yes, even Esau, who will sell his birthright for an evening meal! Faith is a hardy gift. Even the best of us treat it badly, and the worst of us treat it abominably, yet faith reasserts itself in places both grand and base.

Faith takes an interesting turn with Jacob. As we follow the unfolding story a little later, we discover that the key son of Jacob proves not to be the eldest, Reuben, or the most attractive and promising, Joseph, but Judah, who is badly smudged along the way. He is key because Israel's greatest king, David, comes through Judah's line, and for Christians it is the line of Judah through which Jesus comes.

Even though Judah will be the family's royal line, and Levi will be the professional family of religious leadership, Joseph is the faith conveyor. Jacob blesses each of Joseph's sons while "bowing in worship over the top of his staff"—a picture of an aged man whose life seems fragile but who exercises his patriarchal privilege and responsibility with all his remaining energy. It seems clear that Jacob saw in Joseph what he couldn't see in Joseph's older brothers—the quality of faith that was the dominant and redeeming feature in his own life.

Joseph showed that faith in a unique way. "By faith Joseph, at the end of his life, made mention of the exodus of the Israelites and gave instructions about his burial"—or about his *bones*, as the footnote translation puts it (Hebrews 11:22). Joseph had come to Egypt unwillingly, sold into slavery by his brothers. He had prospered there—prospered to the degree that he named one of his sons Manasseh, meaning, "God has made me forget all my hardship and all my father's house" (Genesis 41:51). It might seem that Joseph, the most honored of Egypt's citizens even though himself a foreigner, was glad to forget his family ties.

Instead, however, he became the instrument in bringing his entire extended family to Egypt, thus saving them from famine. It would have been easy for the family to settle in and make Egypt their permanent home. Egypt had culture, refinements of civilization, and comforts not to be found in the pasturelands where the family of Israel had been dwelling. A popular song after World War I asked how America would keep its boys "down on the farm" after they had seen Paris. The principle was likely to be persuasively at work with the family of Israel. Indeed, even after suffering generations of Egyptian slavery and escaping under Moses' leadership, the Israelites mourned at times for the food and security of Egypt. All of which is to say that it would have been very easy—in fact, entirely natural—for the family of Israel to forget that there was a divine claim on their lives, a claim carried from Abraham to Isaac to Jacob. And if they had forgotten, they would have intermarried with the Egyptians and would never have become a nation.

It was Joseph who planted the seed of faith in the family. As he died he said to his brothers, "I am about to die; but God will surely come to you, and bring you up out of this land to the land that he swore to Abraham, to Isaac, and to Jacob." Then Joseph forced an oath on his family before dying: "When God comes to you, you shall carry up my bones from here." He died, and "he was embalmed and placed in a coffin in Egypt" (Genesis 50:24-26). And when Israel left Egypt generations later, the people were faithful. The biblical writer tells us, "And Moses took with him the bones of Joseph who had required a solemn oath of the Israelites, saying, 'God will surely take notice of you, and then you must carry my bones with you from here'" (Exodus 13:19). Joseph had been dead for several centuries, according to the biblical record, but through those centuries his body had been a mute witness to the promise given to Abraham, Isaac, and Jacob. Joseph's bones were not to be left in Egypt. The promise to Israel was that their homeland was to be in Canaan, and Joseph, the spiritual heir to the patriarchs, wanted to be sure that his body was carried to its spiritual home.

Faith has its physical symbols. You and I are physical creatures so we need the reminder that physical symbols bring. For some it is a family Bible, for some a cherished stained-glass window, for many a particular song, and for some a pocket ornament. I no longer choose to disparage anyone's faith symbol if it evokes godly responses and a more effective walk with God. Joseph did not want his bones to reside permanently anywhere except in the land of promise. He lived more than three quarters of his life in Egypt, but his faith tied him to the land of promise.

Faith is carried in an exotic variety of receptacles. Some seem unworthy of their assignment. A critic will dispose of some as "childish" and others as "mere sentiment" and still others as "silly." But the judgment is not mine to make. If the receptacle conveys faith to the end of holy living, I will honor it as I do the donkey that carried our Lord into Jerusalem at the beginning of the week we call "Holy."

I will never cease marveling at the ways faith can be communicated from one generation to the next or one person to the next. William Purcell was a young advertising man in London, wrapped up in his career, when

> suddenly, one lunch-hour, when the pigeons were feeding in the sun in Lincoln's Inn, at a spot I can identify to this day, there came upon me, with a genuine shock, the realization that if no motive or higher purpose or aim could be discovered in life beyond the mere persistence in it, then the game was simply not worth the candle. I cannot now recall whether there was any particular incident which triggered off this explosion of thought . . . but it was the result which counted.[1]

So it is that faith is sometimes carried in Joseph's bones, sometimes in a hymn, and sometimes in a ritual that is foolish to one and beautiful to another. Sometimes faith comes via the life of a saint and sometimes through a human so unlikely that one feels the Holy Spirit must that day have chosen the carrier in error. Somehow faith is communicated; another person, another generation, believes: Abraham, Isaac, and Jacob, and the bones of Joseph.

Some years after Joseph was gone, as the book of Exodus reports it, "a new king arose over Egypt, who did not know Joseph" (Exodus 1:8). For that new king, the family of Israel was nothing other than a military threat, people who might someday cooperate with an invading army. Thus the family that had once been held in esteem because of their kinsman, Joseph, became a group best controlled by putting it under a system of slavery. "But the more they were oppressed, the more they multiplied" (Exodus 1:12), and so too grew the fear and hatred of the Egyptians until they concluded that the only way to protect themselves against this threat was to order the death of all the boy babies.

Once again there was someone of faith: a man from the house of Levi who was married to a Levite woman. They had a son who was such a "fine baby" that they disobeyed the king's command and hid him for three months (Exodus 2:2). Eventually the mother entrusted him to a papyrus basket placed in the reeds of the river where his sister could watch him from a distance and where eventually the daughter of Pharaoh discovered him. She adopted him, named him Moses, and raised him with royal privileges. We'll speak more of him later, but for now we pause only long enough to ponder the communicating of faith. How is it that this couple from the tribe of Levi had the courage to defy the king's command and then trust the child to the waters of the Nile? Where did they get such faith? Many generations removed from Abraham, Isaac, and Jacob, how is it that they had the faith to watch over the life of the one who would eventually lead Israel from slavery and who would fulfill Joseph's command to bring his bones from Egypt to the land of promise? How is it that faith of such quality was alive and communicable over such a long period of time and in such inhospitable circumstances?

Then there is an even more perplexing story, that of the woman Rahab. We will deal with her story, too, in more detail a little later, but I must speak of her just now because she is a particular example of faith being communicated unreasonably and against the odds.

When the fledgling nation of Israel set out to conquer Canaan, its first obstacle was the ancient walled city of Jericho. Israel's leader, Joshua, sent two men ahead secretly to "view the land, especially Jericho" (Joshua 2:1). The two men chose to stay in the house of a prostitute, Rahab. Her house was on the city wall—a wall made of two separate walls with a space of about ten feet between, some of which was used for storage and some for dwellings. Such a location was advantageous for a prostitute because it made access easy for travelers. The biblical writer says nothing about the relationship between the two Israelites and Rahab except to note that they "spent the night there" (Joshua 2:1).

Meanwhile the king of Jericho heard about the spies and sent orders to Rahab to turn them over. She chose to tell the king's messengers that the men had already left, and she proceeded to hide them in the stalks of flax on her flat rooftop until it was dark enough for them to escape safely down the side of the wall by her house. But before they left, she—of all things—confessed her faith in the God of Israel. "I know that the LORD has given you the land," she said. "The LORD your God is indeed God in heaven above and on earth below" (Joshua 2:9, 11). She then asked their pledge to preserve her and her family when Israel took Jericho.

So it is that centuries later the New Testament writer includes Rahab in the faith hall of fame: "By faith Rahab the prostitute did not perish with those who were disobedient, because she had received the spies in peace" (Hebrews 11:31). Rahab was a kind of Noah, saving her own extended family from the destruction that wiped out all the rest of Jericho. It was "by faith" that she did so, the writer reports, and she demonstrated her faith by receiving the spies "in peace"—that is, she protected them from the death that would no doubt have been inflicted on them as war spies.

It was a dangerous thing to do. People who protect spies are seen as enemies of their country. They are usually despised within their own extended family. The chances of being detected were high. Rahab was asking for trouble—very possibly for a death penalty if she were caught. So why did she take on herself such a peril? She did it "by faith." She had heard, as had others in her nation, about this strange body of runaway slaves who had escaped from Egypt some forty years before and who were now, at last, a threat to the land of Canaan.

If we put these pieces together in fairly logical fashion, we calculate that the Israelites fled Egypt before Rahab was born. No doubt legends had grown around the original story, especially with the lapse of years before Israel appeared as a military threat. Somehow Rahab was convinced that the Israelites were invincible, because "the LORD [had] given [them] the land," and that this God whom they worshiped was not like the regional gods and the various nature gods with which the people of Jericho were familiar; this was a God, Rahab said, who was "in heaven above and on earth below."

So here is our question: how is it that Rahab had such faith? Had folktales gotten out of hand so that the prostitute of Jericho was caught up in some childish superstition? The writer of Hebrews didn't think so. He saw Rahab as a woman of faith, someone to be mentioned in the same series of notables as Noah, Abraham, and Moses.

But where did she get her faith? We can understand how Isaac got his from his father, Abraham, and how Jacob got it from his father and his grandfather before him. But how does a woman of Jericho, resident of a city that had gods of its own, come to have faith in the Lord God of Israel? I may not have to explain Rahab's story to you because you may have within your own life or family a good enough story of someone who, against the odds, came to know of Christ and a new way of life. You may have wondered often enough about the kind of grace that found someone with no traceable spiritual heritage who nevertheless became a person of faith.

If so, I don't need to convince you that faith is communicable—and that sometimes the Spirit of God communicates faith in ways that seem wonderful and beyond easy explanation. In such a circumstance you may have decided that explanation is not as important as giving thanks—thanks for the communicating of faith.

Above all, remember this: the communicating of faith is not your business alone—or mine. Nor is it a business restricted to the church and to certified religious institutions. Faith was conveyed in Israel by a body that the people held sacred, and in Jericho by a woman who was moved by the rumors that had reached her, probably through the customers that had come to her marginal life, and in modern London where the pigeons were eating in the noonday sun.

The Holy Spirit helps with the communication. God's Spirit is at work in this business of communicating faith, because God's stake in faith is greater even than our own.

CHAPTER NINE

Faith Has the Long View

Scripture Reading: Hebrews 11:24-28

I'd like for everything I say or write about faith to inspire you. I realize that we live in a world where it's often difficult to keep believing because the voices against faith are loud and strong. It's difficult in such a world to fight against the prevailing tide. Part of that prevailing tide is the culture of impatience. We expect everything to happen *now*. See how upset most of us get when the computer takes extra seconds to warm up. Well, this impatience that surrounds us, this culture of the immediate, affects our faith life, too. In the church of my boyhood the congregation loved to sing "We'll Understand It Better By and By," but they were used to waiting. We're not. When my parents' generation was reminded that a day with the Lord is as a thousand years, they said "amen" and took a new grip on life. We wonder why we have to wait until tomorrow morning.

That brings us to the issue of this lesson in faith. Like it or not, if I'm honest I have to tell you that faith has the long view. This is the back side of faith, but it's also the front side, and the top and bottom too, so we might as well get with it.

Faith is a work of art—a work of *spiritual* art—and art is almost never a quick production. I remember the Christian cartoonist whose small son asked one day if God helped him with his drawing, and when he replied in the affirmative, his son asked, "Then why do you have to erase so much?" Faith is not easy. For most of us, most of the time, it involves a good deal of trial and error, with erasing as the norm. In time we learn that some of the smudges on our faith canvas transform the background into the beautiful setting that it is: the setting for the grandeur of the picture's key scene. But it doesn't come easily.

I think I could make my point about faith and the long view by way of any of the faith heroes referred to in Hebrews 11. I've chosen Moses, however, because the way he exercised the long view relates to the practicing values of the culture in which most of us live. You know from your earlier reading that Moses' life was miraculously spared because of the faith of his parents and his older sister, and that the little Hebrew boy who was doomed by the king's command became instead an inhabitant of a palace as the adopted son of the king's daughter.

We're not given any real details about those growing-up years, but it's not hard to fill in some of the gaps. When Stephen, the first Christian martyr, summarized the story of God's dealings with the people of Israel, he said simply that Pharaoh's daughter adopted Moses "and brought him up as her own son. So Moses was instructed in all the wisdom of the Egyptians and was powerful in his words and deeds" (Acts 7:21-22). At that time Egypt was ahead of the parade in art and learning, and when Stephen says that Pharaoh's daughter brought Moses up "as her own son," it's clear that he got the best. After all, for the king's grandson to get anything less would reflect on the king.

Above all, the life that Moses knew in his royal setting was a life of privilege. Kings by tradition have seen themselves—and have been seen by their subjects—as inherent objects of favor. It's a favor to which kings were born, and even in instances where their talents were slight, they were seen as if they were significant. I'm sure this was especially true in an ancient time, among people to which the concepts of freedom and human equality were essentially unknown. In cultures where there were many gods, a king was seen as one of the gods and thus was to be feared not only for his political power but even more for his godly status. To grow up in such an atmosphere, such philosophical air, was to grow up thinking of oneself as not necessarily privileged, but as simply enjoying one's inherent rights. This was the mind-set of Moses' world. Such a mind-set can intoxicate even a very sober soul.

But there was more to Moses than the culture in which he was raised. Perhaps someday psychiatry and psychology—or some derivative studies not yet imagined—will tell us the measure to which we are influenced by what goes on in the first months of our lives, how we are influenced by the experience of birth, and even how we are shaped by our residence in the womb. A very earthy wisdom, the type that peasants know, has been expressed from time immemorial; for example, in the phrase that there are things we "drink in with our mother's milk." Ancient people, including the Hebrews, believed that ethnic continuity and solidarity came with an infant's suckling and that it was therefore important that a child be nurtured at the right ethnic breast.

See then how carefully the writer of Exodus unfolds a particular detail in the story of Moses' infancy. His parents have seen that he is "a fine baby" and therefore they dare to defy the king's command that all male Hebrew babies should be killed at birth. They raise their son in secrecy for three months, until they can hide him no longer, and then put him in a papyrus basket among the reeds in the hope some kind Egyptian will spare him. They position his sister Miriam to watch him from a place in hiding. A kind Egyptian does, indeed, find him—the king's daughter. The baby "was crying, and she took pity on him" (Exodus 2:6).

So what do you do when a baby cries? You feed him! At this point Miriam stepped forward. "Shall I go and get you a nurse from the Hebrew women to nurse the child for you?" Pharaoh's daughter answered, "Yes," and Miriam "called the child's mother." The princess instructed her, " 'Take this child and nurse it for me, and I will give you your wages.' So the woman took the child and nursed it" (Exodus 2:7-9). In a few short sentences we are told three times about the nursing of the child, beginning with Miriam's offer to get a *Hebrew* woman to nurse the child. This was a suggestion with political and social appeal, because an Egyptian woman wouldn't want to nurse a Hebrew child. But it was also ensuring that the child's suckling would be at a Hebrew breast—and more particularly, at the breast of his birth mother. The biblical writer wants us to know that something very human, somewhat mystical, and altogether powerful is happening with this child.

How much are we products of our ancestry and how much of our environment? The discussion will never come to an end, probably because the two intertwine so intricately that we don't know where one leaves off and the other begins. In Moses' story the crisis of ancestry and environment comes when he is forty years old. The number forty is symbolic in biblical usage, representing a period of training and testing; in this case, the period is over and Moses is ready to enter a new phase of life. Exodus puts it this way: "One day, after Moses had grown up, he went out to his people and saw their forced labor" (Exodus 2:11). He has "grown up" enough to recognize that these slaves are "his people" and to see some things that previously I think he was not able to comprehend. It is a grand moment when you hear music where previously there was only sound, when you see loveliness where once the object was ordinary, and where you feel responsibility when before you enjoyed objective distance.

This is the moment the New Testament writer has in mind when he writes, "By faith Moses, when he was grown up [this writer, like the writer of Exodus, knows that Moses has "grown up" to spiritual maturity] refused to be called a son of Pharaoh's daughter, choosing rather to share ill-treatment with the people of God than to enjoy the fleeting pleasures of sin" (Hebrews 11:24-25).

This is where Moses begins to learn that faith has a *long view*— longer by far than he could ever have anticipated when the faith-urging first ignited his soul. Moses' motives were noble the day he reacted so violently to the brutality of the Egyptian overseer that he killed him. I doubt that at that moment he had any long-range plan in mind. In any event, he discovered the next day that he had started something he wasn't ready or able to carry through, and on that day he embarked on a very long journey—eighty years, the writer of Exodus tells us—that still left him only on the border of fulfillment.

It was a strange journey. The favored inheritor of royal privilege became a fugitive. The man exquisitely trained to lead other men and women, which no doubt would have included some role in government, became a sheepherder. He spent forty years sheepherding, in fact. After that he endured an intense period of confrontation with a powerful ruler—Egypt's Pharaoh may well have been the most significant leader of the time—and then spent some forty years leading a generally ungrateful people through their growing-up and growing-together period. The man who had been trained for sophisticated conversation was assigned to guide a wavering crowd of nomads in their basic need for daily food and water. And he had another job for which he had probably received no preparation: he had to learn how to keep these people encouraged and hopeful through long years when their goal was not in sight.

But Moses had faith. It was in his blood. He had drunk it in with his infant milk. He came from hardy faith stock: his parents had spared and protected his life by faith, and had somehow conveyed the rudiments of that faith to him. Thus when he looked out on his kin—slaves whose way of life was so different from his own palace life that he had to wonder what connection there could possibly be between himself and these people who were more like pack animals than human beings—he knew that he must do something about their misery.

Where did Moses get such a humanitarian impulse? I'd like to make at least a minor case for his stepmother, the king's daughter. There was something very good in that woman that made her adopt an alien baby in direct contradiction to government policy—a policy her own father enunciated. I think the attitude of this unnamed woman influenced Moses in some measure, just as I observe that many of us get part of our social and economic conscience from people who may seem to have little religious motivation.

However, generally such admirable impulses assert themselves only in limited ways. They rarely become the driving issue of our lives. It's too easy to rationalize, to convince ourselves that society's problem is not our problem—the situation is dire, yes, and something ought to be done, yes, but we're not the ones to do it. Something, however, compelled Moses to endanger his life and his comfortable existence on an act of justice. It was angry justice, as the spirit of justice often is, and it was certainly not thought through. As we have said, Moses had no plan. All he had was a momentary rush of righteous anger. He acted on it, and within twenty-four hours he had lost everything.

That's how Moses got himself into the wilderness, with no career, no predictable future, and no use for the education and refinement that had been bred into him during his years of royal privilege. There he existed for forty years, on the back side of nowhere, tending sheep, raising a family, and conversing with his father-in-law (who was fortunately a quite admirable figure). Nevertheless, there was no future for Moses—none, at least, that would fire the soul of such a man.

This is where I raise a question. During the forty years that Moses was tending sheep for his father-in-law, did he remember the privileges of Egyptian royal life, and did he ask himself how he could have fallen so far? Did he think of luxurious rooms and curtained beds and many-course meals, with servants always at the raising of an imperial finger? Did he remember the fragrance of food prepared by the nation's best chefs?

The New Testament writer thinks he did. When the writer says that Moses "refused to be called a son of Pharaoh's daughter, choosing rather to share ill-treatment with the people of God than to enjoy the fleeting pleasures of sin" (Hebrews 11:24-25), I note that he knew what he was giving up: the "pleasures of sin"— a life of indolence, of privilege without price, of benefits without requirements.

I notice also the adjective that describes those pleasures: they were "fleeting." Somehow Moses knew that these were pleasures that would not last because they could not. They were without substance. Moses had the faith to know that those pleasures, though they were highly tangible—food, sensual indulgence, endless entertainment—were not real. They had no eternal substance. They were *fleeting*. They couldn't last. You thought you had them in hand, and then you saw there was nothing there.

Well, that's a grand revelation. But how does it hold for forty years of tending sheep? The day the call came, the new step in Moses' life, the sheepherding former royal personality argued with God.

Faith doesn't always come in grand declarations. Sometimes it travels into the soul by way of wrestling with God and conscience and conflicting desires and perhaps just plain ennui. We find it easier to stay where we are, in the known, rather than venture into the uncertainties of the unknown. Maybe the solitude of the desert, the security of his family, and the occasional evenings of philosophical discussion with his father-in-law had dulled Moses' sense for the larger issues. Or perhaps years of sheep tending had broken Moses' spirit so that he couldn't imagine himself in any other role. So he argued with God.

Eventually Moses lost his argument and won his calling. What followed was a series of confrontations with a potentate who could at any moment have taken Moses' life; dealing with a people held together by their ethnic roots and by their community of slavery but with no perception of what freedom and self-government would be; and then a generation of wandering in the wilderness—back to sheepherding, verily, except that these sheep talked back.

He did this, the writer of Hebrews says, because he had faith that this was better than "the fleeting pleasures of sin." He had the long view—the long view that comes with faith.

But he didn't know how long it would be. Because on the way he became impatient—with his people, for sure, and perhaps indirectly with God—and in his impatience he violated his walk with God to the point that God said Moses would never enter the land of promise. As Moses' story ends, he stands on a mountain where he can see the land to which he has been leading Israel for forty years—and philosophically, the land for which he embarked forty years before that when he killed the Egyptian taskmaster in a moment of righteous anger. But he doesn't get to enter the land.

His people, in their second generation, will enter it, but he will only see it from afar, though with "sight [that] was unimpaired" and with "vigor [that] had not abated" (Deuteronomy 34:7). The long view, indeed.

Moses' faith view was so long, in fact, that the New Testament writer is sure Moses saw centuries ahead. Thus he writes, "He [Moses] considered abuse suffered for the Christ to be greater wealth than the treasures of Egypt, for he was looking ahead to the reward" (Hebrews 11:26). As we read that we're likely to ask how Christ got into this Old Testament story. Well, this is the long view of faith with which the New Testament writer looks at everything in the Old Testament story. For the writer of Hebrews, the end of Moses' story is not in the land of Canaan, and certainly not on the mountain where he died; it is in Christ, and in the church, and in the someday-fulfilled kingdom of God. The writer of Hebrews is not only sure of what Moses was doing when, at age forty, he turned his back on the fleeting pleasures of Egypt and began his role as Israel's deliverer and lawgiver, but is also sure that Moses saw the eventual consummation in Christ.

That's the long view. And only faith can grasp it, for Moses, for you, or for me.

CHAPTER TEN

Faith's Heroes
Are a Mixed Lot

Scripture Reading: Hebrews 11:31-32

As I read this wonderful eleventh chapter of Hebrews I sense at a certain point that the writer feels he's running out of time—perhaps like the preacher who suddenly notices that it's already one minute until noon and that if he doesn't abbreviate his closing point the congregation will be done before he is. So our biblical writer, knowing he hasn't time to give us detailed stories, begins simply to list names, trusting that his readers will know enough biblical history to attach events to the names. Then he reverses the method by listing grand acts of heroism anonymously, leaving it to us to remember who did them. We recognize some of these incidents and attach a name, but others are rather generally inclusive and details are left to our imagination. All told, the process provides us with a quite heterogeneous collection.

"And what more should I say?" he asks, and lists six names plus a general category ("the prophets"), all the while apologizing,

"For time would fail me to tell of . . ." I know the feeling. Nevertheless, I ask myself—as perhaps you do—about some of the names he leaves out. Since he mentions the judge Barak, why doesn't he mention Barak's more articulate and probably stronger partner, Deborah? It isn't sexual prejudice, else he wouldn't have included Sarah and Rahab. Since he mentions David, why not include Jonathan, whose faith in God's purposes was so great that he gladly stepped back from his own potential because he believed God wanted David rather than him as Israel's king? And how can you settle for "the prophets" and not mention specifically Elijah, who could stare down hundreds of pagan opponents, or Jeremiah, who by faith courageously suffered mistreatment from kings and commoners alike?

Perhaps you'd like to tell me that it's none of my business or that I'm tampering with divine inspiration (which is not really my intention); but however and why ever, I come back to my earlier statement: the writer gives us a mixed lot.

Let's start with Rahab. We won't spend much time with her because we mentioned her earlier in another connection. It almost seems as if the writer's reference to her in verse 31 got him going in an adverse direction. "By faith Rahab the prostitute did not perish with those who were disobedient, because she had received the spies in peace" (Hebrews 11:31). You can't help noticing that the writer refers to Rahab's profession without apology or explanation. He's as matter-of-fact as if he were saying, "Rahab the seamstress." She was a prostitute; this is what she was, no more, no less. And the biblical writer doesn't seem the least surprised that God used her, nor is he troubled by God's choice.

In the song "Is There for Honest Poverty" by Robert Burns there is a line about "a man's a man for all of that," and it seems as if the writer is treating Rahab the same way, as if to say, "Faith is faith, whoever exercises it."

Then see what follows. The list begins with four judges from that worrisome period when the young nation of Israel was struggling to establish itself in its new homeland. Those were rugged days, not for the faint of heart or for those with effete taste. I can't find a plan in the order in which the names appear; they're neither logical nor chronological. The first in the list is Gideon. When the angel of the Lord approaches Gideon in the biblical story, he addresses him as "you mighty warrior," which makes you feel that the angel has a sense of humor because at that moment Gideon is in hiding, beating out his wheat in a wine press because he fears the Midianites.

For a while Gideon does nothing to change this impression of cowardice. To his credit, he knows his nation's history well enough to remind the angel that God blessed Israel in the good old days—so why not now? The angel promptly puts the ball back in Gideon's court: "Go in this might of yours and deliver Israel." Gideon continues in his pusillanimous mood: "But sir, how can I deliver Israel? My clan is the weakest in Manasseh [his tribe], and I am the least in my family" (Judges 6:15). I don't think this is a solicitous act of humility, the kind that seeks to elicit a compliment. Gideon would really rather continue beating his grain in hiding.

Gideon continues to argue and to ask for signs, and the angel is patient. But when at last Gideon agrees to go, we see that he was wise to object as long as he did. When thirty-two thousand men answer Gideon's call, the Lord says it is too many, and when the number is reduced to ten thousand, it is still too many. A little assemblage of three hundred men, each equipped with a trumpet, a torch, and a jar, finally wins the victory. It is a faith victory, no doubt about it. And Gideon's faith is all the more impressive in light of a personality that seems at first to be cautious if not flat-out timid. Gideon disappoints us later in his life, but unfortunate as that is, it isn't entirely surprising. Even the most unlikely heroes easily come to think that they're rather special, as Gideon did.

Barak belongs in this list of faith heroes, but as I've already indicated, it seems that his coleader, Deborah, should be here, too. They were a duo act, and nobody wanted more for it to be that way than Barak. It was another of those times when Israel was under the rule of a neighboring power, a condition that makes up most of the plot of the book of Judges. This was an especially hopeless time because King Jabin of Canaan had nine hundred chariots of iron, which suggests that Jabin's kingdom was one of the most militarily advanced of his time. And within his kingdom he was a mean man—he "had oppressed the Israelites cruelly twenty years" (Judges 4:3).

But Israel had come to its spiritual senses enough to know that it needed God's help, so they "cried out to the LORD." Enter Deborah. She was a prophetess and a judge in Israel, a person impressive in her ability, strength of character, and wisdom. One wonders how it was that in a time and place when women had few rights and no offices, Deborah had this double calling—

spiritual and political. From a biblical point of view she was the complete person for national leadership, and somehow the people had recognized Deborah's gifts.

She chose, however, to solicit help from Barak, a man from the tribe of Naphtali. But *solicit* is the wrong word. Listen to how she greeted Barak: "The LORD, the God of Israel, commands you" (Judges 4:6). Nothing timid about that! We don't know anything about Barak's background or training, beyond his father's name and his tribal tie, but it is clear that he was wise. He answered Deborah, "If you will go with me, I will go; but if you will not go with me, I will not go" (4:8). Deborah agreed readily but with the warning that the road on which he was going would not bring him glory; glory would be given "into the hand of a woman." The prediction is wonderfully apt. Jael, wife of Heber, a Kenite, killed the enemy general with her own hammer and tent peg when he was fleeing from Barak and Deborah.

Barak and Deborah then sang a song of victory and thanksgiving. The chapter heading in my Bible calls it "The Song of Deborah," but the Scripture itself tells us that Deborah and Barak sang it together. I suspect that Deborah sang the melody and Barak the harmony. I like Barak very much, even though I've questioned why the writer of Hebrews doesn't mention both persons, especially when Deborah was almost surely the dominant personality. But perhaps that's just the point. I remind us of what I said in the story of Abraham and Sarah—that sometimes it takes more faith to follow God as the secondhand recipient than as the initial recipient of the call. Barak is in the Sarah role: God gives orders to Deborah and she passes them on to Barak. I like

Barak's wisdom—the wisdom that comes from humility (and there's very little genuine wisdom that isn't riven through by humility). Nor is Barak put off by the warning that he will not receive glory from the victory. Some wise person has said that untold good could be done in our world if no one cared who got the credit. Barak was such a person. The more I think about it, the more I'm glad that Barak's name is in this catalog of faith greatness. There is a quality of holiness in his faith that I find truly awesome. And we have no record of his falling into the ego trap that caught Gideon.

Then there's Samson. I hardly need to tell his story, because when you're handsome, athletic, and devastatingly attractive to women—and attracted to them in turn—you don't need a public relations man, except to temper the gossip. The hand of God was on Samson before he was born. His father seems a little on the dull side, but his mother makes up for it. Samson would have been huge in our day because he would have made headlines in both the sports publications and the tabloids. More than that, he would have been on the front page in the political news as well, because his feats of strength were constantly humiliating Israel's then primary enemy, the Philistines.

So what does Samson have to do with faith? First, that faith is clearly the secret of his strength. Samson's mother is so advised before her son's birth; he is to be dedicated uniquely to the Lord. And when late in his ill-managed career he has forfeited his strength, he regains it for one last act of bravado by way of a penitent's prayer, which is very much a cry of faith.

But something else in Samson's story impresses me even more. Erratic as he was, and irresponsible in the use of his remarkable gifts, he somehow continued to be touched by the Holy Spirit. While he was still a boy the "spirit of the LORD began to stir him" (Judges 13:25), and repeatedly in his strange career as strong man and national leader "the spirit of the LORD rushed on him" (Judges 14:6, 19; 15:14). Samson seemed to know that his super strength was a gift from God, and he exercised it by faith. When, on the other hand, he presumed on God, the strength was not there (Judges 16:20-21). Although faith is a gift, it is not to be used indiscriminately or arrogantly. Samson demonstrated that faith is not synonymous with self-confidence, and he did it in his own unique way.

Jephthah is one of the most tragic figures in the Scriptures, but he too has his place in faith's hall of fame. The King James Version introduces him with stark eloquence: "Now Jephthah the Gileadite was a mighty man of valour, and he was the son of an harlot" (Judges 11:1). Driven out of his father's home when he was hardly more than a boy, he developed remarkable gifts of leadership and eventually delivered Israel from the oppression of the Amorites; but by an ill-conceived oath he sacrificed his own daughter to his victory. Jephthah consistently recognized that his ability was a gift from God, and he challenged the gods of his opponents in a fashion that would have pleased Elijah.

Jephthah was an irregular character in almost every way. By usual judgment he was ill born, gifted in his ability to draw all kinds of people to himself, thoughtful in diplomacy, and possessed a faith that had elements of superstition, yet he believed in

God's ultimate purposes for his nation. But he was irregular, no doubt about that.

Now the writer of Hebrews turns to more conventional personalities—not perfect, mind you, for the Scriptures are too honest to paint their characters with an immaculate brush. But when we find David and Samuel in the list, we are not surprised. True, David was guilty of deception on occasions, and he was guilty of adultery with the wife of Uriah and arranged for Uriah's death; and in the latter years of his kingship he had an attack of ego that cost his nation dearly. However, he was also a man who knew how to pray and who honored the Lord and was committed to obedience.

I see David's faith, especially, in two expressions. When King Saul became David's enemy, he led a body of his troops to apprehend David and to destroy him. Twice during this period David had the opportunity to kill Saul. In both cases David's aides insisted that God had delivered Saul into his hands—just the kind of reasoning we humans delight in—but David replied that he could not "raise his hand against the LORD's anointed."

Then there were those instances where David so readily saw his guilt. When the prophet Nathan confronted the king on his sin with Bathsheba, David didn't replace him with a new court prophet; rather, he repented, with a fierce sense of his sin. And when he was fleeing the palace under the revolt of his own handsome son, Absalom, and a relative of Saul mocked David and threw stones at him, David stopped his guards from attacking the man: "Let him alone, and let him curse; for the LORD has bidden him" (2 Samuel 16:11). And near the end of his career, when his pride brought disaster to the nation, David took full responsibility and pleaded with God, "I alone have sinned, and I alone have done wickedly; but these sheep, what have they done? Let your hand, I pray, be against me and against my father's house" (2 Samuel 24:17).

David teaches us, by his example, that faith is woven through with humility and repentance. If there is anything that stands out in David's life more than his dramatic sins, it is the passionate quality of his repentance. Some of the ill we do cannot be undone, but it can be turned to the shaping of holy character. As a boy in Sunday school I was in awe of David's faith in defeating Goliath. As a man grown older, I am in much greater awe of David's faith made pure in sorrow over his sins.

Samuel is the man who anointed David to his kingship. He is also the last person identified by name in the roll call of faith heroes in Hebrews 11. He came to know God when he was a kind of altar boy in the temple, at a time when "the word of the LORD was rare" and "visions were not widespread" (1 Samuel 3:1). Samuel is the person who served as judge over Israel in some of the nation's darkest days, and he held the people together by prayer. And when his own time of leadership came to an end, he pledged to the nation, "Moreover as for me, far be it from me that I should sin against the LORD by ceasing to pray for you; and I will instruct you in the good and right way" (1 Samuel 12:23). Samuel was the one who transitioned the people of Israel from a government under regional judges to a monarchy under first Saul and then David.

Samuel lived through very different but largely perilous times, when the nation was politically unsettled, often dominated by foreign powers, and unpredictable in its commitment to God; but he remained steadfast. He is the essence of faith that cannot be shaken.

Then, the writer of Hebrews tells us, there were "the prophets" (Hebrews 11:32). One thinks (as I have already mentioned) of people like Elijah and Jeremiah, and, of course, of Isaiah, Ezekiel, Amos, Hosea, Zephaniah, and Malachi, who are known to us by the books that bear their names. But there are also women like the prophetess Huldah, whom the priests consulted in a crucial time in King Josiah's reign (2 Kings 22:14-20), and men like the prophet Michaiah, who dared to contradict the wishes of kings (2 Chronicles 18).

All of them seem larger than life. Kings do not frighten them; entrenched wealth only arouses their righteous wrath; religious authorities don't impress them. Even the grand traditions of Judaism can't escape their scorn: the prophet Amos tells the "house of Israel" that God has said, "I despise your festivals, / and I take no delight in your solemn assemblies." What does God want? "Let justice roll down like waters, / and righteousness like an everflowing stream" (Amos 5:21, 24). One must believe fiercely in principle and integrity to be so indifferent to all of the political, economic, and religious power structures.

See what a sometimes grand, sometimes motley, sometimes courageous, and sometimes vacillating coterie we have in this body of faith heroes! Of those we've referred to in this chapter, one is a prostitute and another the son of a prostitute; another,

however, is a child born to a praying mother who gave her boy
Samuel to God as soon as possible after he was weaned. That boy,
Samuel, is exemplary of a long lifetime of serving God, while
Samson, the son of another admirable and spiritually sensitive
woman, is as unpredictable as a spring breeze. Barak seems to be
a generally honorable man with admirable regard for his col-
league Deborah, but he doesn't strike one as a dynamic leader.

Yet the New Testament writer, looking back on their stories,
sees them all as persons of such faith that we should seek to imi-
tate them. I believe the writer of Hebrews. In fact, I am encouraged by him. If these persons have been elected into God's faith
hall of fame, you and I ought to rise up out of our chairs of resig-
nation and start marching to Zion. There's room for us, too.

CHAPTER ELEVEN

Faith Makes Us Tough

Scripture Reading: Hebrews 11:33-38

Do I make you uneasy by using the word *tough* in a religious book, a book that perhaps you're reading in your devotional hour? Does it seem not only untheological but also in poor taste? I understand your discomfort. I come across the word now and then in the sports section of the newspaper, where it seems more at home—especially with basketball coaches who insist that the only thing their teams lack is *toughness*: they aren't ready to dive on the floor for a loose basketball or to stand unflinching while an opponent charges toward them at a speed that astonishes me. But the more I think about such a sports scene, something in my soul says that *tough* is more appropriate to a discussion of biblical faith than to even the most breathtaking of athletic performances.

Because while games last for four quarters or for nine innings, biblical faith is for a lifetime—or as much of a life as is left when one signs on with God. And biblical faith doesn't usually allow any time-outs. Indeed, after a while we learn that just when we think the opposition is resting, we're blindsided by a new attack.

Biblical faith often compels us to wrestle with forces that are almost impossible to define. We wish sometimes that the opposition to our faith were something we could lay our hands on or strike with some weapon. Instead, the adversary is hard even to comprehend, let alone attack in any physical form.

You'll understand my point best if you'll join me again at the eleventh chapter of the Letter to the Hebrews. After the writer has named some of the great faith-souls from times past, he summarizes the heroic conduct that has characterized these persons as well as some others whom he has never clearly mentioned.

> For the time would fail me to tell of . . . [those] who through faith conquered kingdoms, administered justice, obtained promises, shut the mouths of lions, quenched raging fire, escaped the edge of the sword, won strength out of weakness, became mighty in war, put foreign armies to flight. Women received their dead by resurrection. Others were tortured, refusing to accept release, in order to obtain a better resurrection. Others suffered mocking and flogging, and even chains and imprisonment. They were stoned to death, they were sawn in two, they were killed by the sword; they went about in skins of sheep and goats, destitute, persecuted, tormented—of whom the world was not worthy. They wandered in deserts and mountains, and in caves and holes in the ground. (Hebrews 11:32-38)

This is no oratorical declaration, listed in categories or with mounting fervor from the less dramatic to the utterly awesome. Rather, it is a kind of conglomerate of wonder. If this message came to us orally rather than in writing, the speaker would sometimes overwhelm us with an avalanche of words and then slip into fretful pauses while wondering just what to say next and how or where to find the words to say it. He is all but breathless in the admiration he feels for these women and men who have held to their faith when everything in the universe has been against them.

We can connect many of these allusions to specific Old Testament persons; one thinks of David, Samson, Daniel, Shadrach, Meshach, Abednego, and a variety of military heroes. Others no doubt refer to courageous figures in the Maccabean struggle for Jewish independence in the second century B.C., out of which came the Jewish commemorative celebration Hanukkah.

Sometimes the list seems strangely broad. One might ask how we can compare "administered justice" and "obtained promises" with being "stoned to death" or "sawn in two." But courage and the faith from which it flows find their own definitions, and they should be held in admiration rather than in comparison or contrast. I think of a battlefield hero who said that gunfire hadn't frightened him as much as making a public statement in defense of a minority person's right to equal housing. Indeed, this biblical catalog of heroism demonstrates the depth and breadth and height of faith. There is a place for faith for women and men, for warriors and administrators, for martyrs and survivors.

However, there's one thing this list doesn't do: it doesn't support the idea that faith always wins—not on this earth, that is. An earnest Christian told me a few days ago that you can't outgive God. If that means there is sublime fulfillment in giving, I agree fully. But if that means if we give dollars we will get back more dollars, well, I part company with that notion, and I dare to say that the writer of Hebrews 11 does, too. I began tithing when

I had one pair of shoes, and now I live in a degree of comfort, so perhaps some would say that I prove that you can't outgive God. But I remember a woman in a small Iowa town where I served as a pastor for a brief period long ago—so long ago that the woman's only income was her pension of twenty-four dollars a month. She had a standing understanding that her pastor would come at a given date each month so that, though homebound, she could give her tithe of two dollars and forty cents. Believe me, it was a modest home. Even though the economy was different in those days, I don't know how she managed. She wasn't rewarded with hundreds of dollars for paying her tithes of just over two dollars. I remember her as rich in the loveliest sense of the word, but her tithing didn't increase her income.

For some, what I am now saying would seem to be not only faith from the back side, but faith from a disappointing and ugly back side. Such persons might even argue that I don't know much about faith, because if I did, I would know that faith is always triumphant. If that is so, then the unknown author of the New Testament book of Hebrews was also misinformed, because as we have just observed, some of the great souls he described didn't come home in a victory parade. True, some "shut the mouths of lions," and some women "received their dead by resurrection"; but there were also those who suffered death by stoning, by being sawn in two, and by the sword. The writer praises the faith of the martyred as gladly as he does the faith of those who were delivered. The score of the ball game or the state of the stock market does not measure the effectiveness of faith.

We're talking about *tough* faith. It is measured not by easy measures of success but by such words as *character*, *nobility*, *gallantry*, and *integrity*—words that seem to have an almost archaic sound in much popular conversation. Marilyn Chandler McEntyre warns, "When a word falls into disuse, the experience goes with it."[1] I don't want such words to be lost from our description of great souls only to be supplanted by words like *successful* or *a winner*. I have nothing against such words if there is substance behind them, but I don't want them to be the final measure. And by all means, I don't want us to see such words as the measure of faith. *Faith* is a tough word, and the people who know it best are the toughest people I know. They are still to be reckoned with after the successful and the winners are gone and forgotten.

The finest embodiment of this kind of faith comes to us in the Old Testament book of Daniel. It may be what the writer of Hebrews 11 had in mind when he spoke of those who "quenched raging fire" (Hebrews 11:34). In the time when the armies of Babylon defeated the nation of Israel, the Babylonians took captive some of Israel's finest youth to be trained by the government for its service—much the way some brilliant scientists might be deployed in our world.

These young men came into trouble, however—faith trouble. A law was passed in Babylon that at a given signal everyone was required to bow down and worship a graven image of the king. The faith law by which these young men lived forbade their bowing down to any graven image; forbade them, in fact, to worship anyone or anything other than the Lord God. However, anyone who disobeyed the king would be executed by burning—by being thrown into a furnace.

Everything was at stake. The young men were aliens who had been given special privileges in a foreign land. They had already proved themselves as promising young scholars, and their professional future was bright. They must also have had some sense of indebtedness to the persons in the Babylonian government who believed in them and had trained them to this point of achievement. All of this was, of course, in addition to their basic human urge to survive—to say nothing of the threat of the brutal form of execution!

The young men possessed great faith. From what we know, their commitment to God was nonnegotiable; they didn't even contemplate bowing down to the image of the king. It's clear, too, that they didn't expect the Babylonian government to make them an exception to the law. They made their case clear to the king: "O Nebuchadnezzar, we have no need to present a defense to you in this matter. If our God whom we serve is able to deliver us from the furnace of blazing fire and out of your hand, O king, let him deliver us. But if not, be it known to you, O king, that we will not serve your gods and we will not worship the golden statue that you have set up" (Daniel 3:16-18).

"*But if not.*" This, believe me, is tough faith. Some translations have the three young men declare that they believe their God is able to deliver them. This one interprets them as saying, "*If* our God is able"; but both agree on the ultimate stand the Israelites are taking: they will not, under any circumstances, bow down to false gods. If we are delivered, fine, *but if not,* it makes no difference. We will not violate our faith.

I rejoice in the faith that seems to produce miracles. As this story unfolds, their faith does also, and as they come out of the furnace "the hair of their heads was not singed, their tunics were not harmed, and not even the smell of fire came from them" (Daniel 3:27). But I would honor their faith just as much if the fire had left them as a pile of ashes. I rejoice not in their deliverance, but in their faith. Their faith is in God, not in results. It is satisfied that God is right and that being true to God is the ultimate issue. If it also culminates in a miracle, that's very lovely, but the miracle is not the proof of the faith. Tough faith cares only incidentally about the results. It cares uniquely about our relationship to God.

We are told that the twentieth century saw more Christian martyrs than any preceding century and probably more than the accumulation of the centuries. Now and then some of us have met persons who survived such persecutions and we marvel at their stories. But don't judge their faith by the fact of their survival; marvel at their readiness not to survive. Marvel at all those who have faith to face persecution, whatever the outcome.

I have seen this "but if not" kind of faith in action at levels other than life and death. I think especially of an executive who became part of my congregation in Cleveland, Ohio. I knew that he had moved to our city from an executive role with a similar institution in New York City. I knew nothing more at the time. As the years passed by I saw frequent evidence of the character with which he did his work, and I rejoiced when he became the chief executive officer of a business that was among the largest in America at the time.

Later his oldest son, a young attorney, told me the rest of the story. His father had come to a crisis of Christian conscience in the New York position. He knew that he could not cooperate with the operation of his firm, so he resigned. To my knowledge, he asked for no miracle; he simply sought another position. In time, it became a very impressive one. His faith showed itself not in his success, but in his decision of character.

Somewhere very long ago I learned a simple poem—the kind that hearing once, one is likely to remember.

> So on I go, not knowing,
> I would not if I might;
> I'd rather walk in the dark with God
> Than go alone in the light;
> I'd rather walk by faith with him
> Than go alone by sight.

Only recently have I learned that these lines were originally part of a hymn written by Philip P. Bliss, the author of a number of familiar hymns that are still widely published and sung more than a century later. I knew that Bliss was one of the most popular composers and poets of his time and that he worked with the well-known evangelistic team of Dwight L. Moody and Ira D. Sankey. I knew, too, that he died tragically when he was only thirty-nine years old. He and his wife were traveling from their home in Pennsylvania to one of his singing engagements in Chicago when a train bridge broke over a river near Ashtabula, Ohio. He was at first able to escape from the water, but when he returned to see if he could save his wife, he was burned in the wreckage.

What I didn't know is that the song to which I've just referred was the last song Philip Bliss ever wrote. A devout person might say that Bliss wrote with divine foresight. A more secular person might say it was a remarkable coincidence. Whatever, Philip Bliss died with the faith he had written and sung. He declared a tough faith when he wrote the hymn, and he died in the confidence his faith had given him. I dare to say that though his life and that of his wife were taken in the darkness of drowning, they both died in the light, with the unique sight faith provides.

Here is something of the wonder of faith. It is as good in the night as in the day, in economic depression or prosperity, in failure or success. It is perfect to live by and indispensable to die by. Thus it isn't surprising that the writer of Hebrews doesn't separate faith stories by the classifications we might use, of "success" and "failure." Whether it is "mighty in war" or "chains and imprisonment," it is still a faith story.

Whatever the story or whoever the faith hero, one thing is sure: they were people "of whom the world was not worthy" (Hebrews 11:38). I agree, and I confess readily that these great souls were tougher than I am. I have a distance to go before I can qualify for even the outskirts of their company.

Nevertheless, I want to add a special word to what the biblical writer has said. Although the world is not worthy of persons such as these, if it weren't for such persons I doubt that the world would be worthy to continue. These are the souls who keep the flame of holy integrity alive. When the world seems ready to die of its own corruption, some of these people appear on the scene. When you're in a conversation about the state of politics or business or religion and for a moment all you can see are the fail-ures of character, then it is, thank God, that someone says, "But we mustn't forget so-and-so. She was a great one!"

And often the "great one" isn't a figure known to history; it's a person known only to the one who is making the point. Most of us have such a person in our spiritual journey. Some of us are blessed with scores, even hundreds, of them—great human beings who have faced their own lions, suffered their own rejec-tions and "floggings," and won their own hidden battles—people of faith.

They are people of *tough* faith, faith that has nothing to do with the scoreboard, faith that knows that the game doesn't end this week—and not necessarily in this lifetime. It's tough enough to ignore all such measures and to hold fast to the character of God.

CHAPTER TWELVE

Faith Sees What Others Cannot

Scripture Reading: Hebrews 11:13-16, 39-40; 12:1-2

*B*lind faith. I wonder how long the two words have been linked together in our common speech—so well linked in fact that we see them as the perfectly wedded noun and adjective. And the words are not limited to the world of religion. Most of us have seen marriages that would not have escaped the divorce courts without blind faith. The worst of what we call "confidence men," those persons who make their living (and often a rather substantial one) by playing with the trust others have in them, have built their careers on the blind faith others show them. The most untiring of what we call parental love often holds on by blind faith and little else. Yes, there is such a thing as blind faith, and one can find it in every area of life—in religion and sports and politics and science and romance, to name just a few.

But quality faith is not blind. It is superior vision. It is able to see what others cannot. And it sees it so well that it holds on against all odds.

The person who gave us the Letter to the Hebrews is only a little way into his magnificent declaration in chapter 11 when he says what for some is a contradiction of what they believe faith to be. Having told us the faith stories of Abel, Enoch, Noah, Abraham, and Sarah, he interrupts his recital abruptly to say,

> All of these died in faith without having received the promises, but from a distance they saw and greeted them. They confessed that they were strangers and foreigners on the earth, for people who speak in this way make it clear that they are seeking a homeland. If they had been thinking of the land that they had left behind, they would have had opportunity to return. But as it is, they desire a better country, that is, a heavenly one. Therefore God is not ashamed to be called their God; indeed, he has prepared a city for them. (Hebrews 11:13-16)

That's quite a statement. Apparently the writer is afraid of the very kind of misconception that still plagues every faith discussion; namely, that faith can be measured by its conquests, its successes, its "bottom lines." So he warns us that these persons whose faith so inspires us—and whose stories he is using to enlist us as people of faith—are all persons who didn't get what their faith had envisioned. They all died, he tells us, without having gotten the promises; but he goes on to tell us that they saw these promises "from a distance" and accepted them. As a result, it was clear to them (and probably to others) "that they were strangers and foreigners on the earth."

These remarkable people made it clear that they were "seeking a homeland"—and their seeking was so intense and so unready for compromise that they never considered turning back. If they had wanted to, he tells us, "they would have had opportunity to return"—that is, they were not under some vow that ordered death to deserters; they always had in their possession a return ticket. It was theirs to use if they wanted to. But they were compelled by their desire for "a better country, that is, a heavenly one." They could see something that others could not see. Abel, Enoch, Noah, Abraham, and Sarah were so different from the culture around them that they saw something none of their contemporaries could seem to grasp. And they could see it so clearly that the huge majority vote of their culture in the opposite direction bothered them not at all.

Of course they had an impressive vote on their side. God agreed with them. In fact, God would have been embarrassed by them if they had settled for anything less than this grand faith; but because they had this far-off look, God was "not ashamed to be called their God."

And no wonder. If the Bible says anything about God, it is that God has faith in the future and that this faith is never discouraged by the way we humans fritter and fail, grumble and rebel. God demonstrates the ability to wait and not grow weary. We are undone by the idea that a day with the Lord is as a thousand years, but in truth we should find new heart in it. It assures us that God will not give up until all is right and "the kingdom of the world has become the kingdom of our Lord / and of his Messiah" (Revelation 11:15). Of course God is pleased with those who have the long view, because the long view is the godly view. When we take the long view we're looking at this universe and its unfolding, sometimes erratic history as God does.

Bible scholars generally agree that the Old Testament says very little about eternal life—at least as Christians understand it or as the devout Pharisees of Jesus' day believed in it. Most of the great Old Testament personalities grasped the future primarily by way of their descendants; thus children were singularly important, especially male children. Here and there in the Hebrew Scriptures there is a hint of faith in the world to come, but it is not a dominant theme—and surely not the kind of theme enunciated by the Easter faith of Christianity.

As the writer of the book of Hebrews looks back on his spiritual ancestors, he credits them with belief in the world to come: "They desire a better country," he writes, "that is, a heavenly one." They believed it so much that they were never fully at home on earth. That great American iconoclast, Henry David Thoreau, insisted a few days before his death, "One world at a time."[1] The faith-people of ancient times found time for two, and the assurance of the future one is what added so wonderfully to their confidence in the value of the present one. They had a sense of holy discontent. This discontent did not make them anxious to find an exit; rather, it drove them to bring to this earth as much as possible of the world to come. In this, it could be said that they were already anticipating Jesus' prayer, "Thy kingdom come . . . on earth as it is in heaven."

When the writer tells us that all of those great ancient souls "died in faith without having received the promises," he was thinking especially of Jesus the Christ. As the New Testament writer sees it, the great souls beginning with Abel had been waiting for Jesus Christ. They didn't know how to describe him, but they knew he was their goal. That special company that the writer of Hebrews refers to simply as "the prophets" (Hebrews 11:32) had the clearest vision of Christ, but all of the faith-driven had him in view, however sketchy their image may have been. This is the ultimate, indefinable quality of this procession—or if you prefer, this lineage—of faith.

The first-century writer wanted his readers to know that these great faith heroes of the past "would not, apart from us, be made perfect" (Hebrews 11:40). He wants us to understand that the great and admirable faith that the ancients had invested in God and in the divine plan had come to consummation in Christ; thus those who had now come to faith in Christ had made "perfect" the unfulfilled faith of the generations past. If those of us who are living after Christ has been revealed do not grasp this faith as our own, then a pall is cast over the faith heroes who have prepared the way for us.

The writer paints a dramatic picture. If you've attended an exciting athletic event or have watched the Olympics on television, you catch the feeling the writer is describing. He sees the present generation of those who believe in Christ as runners in a grand race, "surrounded by so great a cloud of witnesses," a crowd-cloud that cheers us on, a crowd made up of all those generations of people who have waited for this consummation to their own faith journey. And because these witnesses have so much at stake in us, the writer urges us to "lay aside every weight and the sin that clings so closely" so that we can "run with perseverance the race that is set before us, looking to Jesus the pioneer and perfecter of our faith, who for the sake of the joy that was set before him endured the cross, disregarding its shame, and has taken his seat at the right hand of the throne of God" (Hebrews 12:1-2).

We noted earlier in our study of faith that the Letter to the Hebrews was written at a time when Christians were suffering persecution and when some—perhaps many—were tempted to forsake the Christian way. The writer wants them (and us) to know that we are being cheered on by the faithful who have preceded us, especially because "apart from us" these great souls from the past would not "be made perfect" (Hebrews 11:40). Abel, Noah, Abraham, Sarah, Moses, and the others all died in faith without seeing the climaxing fulfillment of their faith, but they were sure that it would come; and now they saw before them the generation of completion. No wonder they're a cloud of expectant witnesses. No wonder they cheer us on!

And above all is "Jesus the pioneer and perfecter of our faith." He has led the way, even to enduring the cross, "disregarding its shame." He, too, is part of the faith procession, its ultimate pioneer and perfecter; but he has completed his part in the journey and now he watches from a "seat at the right hand of the throne of God." All of us who believe are part of this grand "race," a race so demanding that those who engage it must "lay aside every weight and the sin that clings so closely," because nothing dare impede our winning this race.

And lest we forget, being a Christian means being *in the race—* not in the stands. Those who have already finished the race are in the stands, cheering us on. Their presence there encourages me tremendously. But you and I are not in the grandstand, and certainly not in some luxury box seat; we're on the track or the playing field.

But back to our issue. This race is for those with the long view, a "long obedience in the same direction," in Friedrich Nietzsche's phrase, because faith is an attitude of obedience. We're too inclined to think of faith as an emotional experience or as a religious virtue; and while faith certainly is found especially in religion, and while it is for sure a virtue, and while it sometimes expresses itself emotionally, the dominant quality of faith-character is one of obedience.

The idea of obedience comes through in the command that we should "run with perseverance the race that is set before us." I like the idea conveyed in *perseverance*; it gives me a feeling of gritting the teeth and refusing to give up. But I also remember the word that is used in the King James Version: *patience*. Run this race with *patience*. Turn over the coin emblazoned "perseverance" and you will see on the other side a rather dull picture. This is patience, and it is as crucial to the quality of faith as is perseverance; they are sides of the same coin. When you and I think of patience we're inclined to think of the virtue we need when we're standing in a checkout line and the person ahead of us delays the process unnecessarily, or when we put up with a person whose style and manner tend to irritate us. But patience at its height is the quality that continues to hold on for the best through months

and years of enduring the worst. It is character for the long pull—
not often glamorous, but altogether dependable.

When we think of any grand and worthy accomplishment we
generally think of the courage shown in some hour of crisis. We
aren't as likely to recall that the crisis times are usually preceded
by seasons of dull, dogged, determined patience. I'm sure that
more battles are lost in the dull and dogged days than in the crisis time. For a period in my pastoral ministry I was the pastor to
several professional football players, some of whom are now in
the National Football League Hall of Fame. I learned that the
spectacular run, the crucial tackle, and the perfect pass were the
product of literally years of *patient* practice. I remember the football player who told me on a quiet afternoon in early summer, "In
a few weeks practice will begin, and from that day on, my body
will not stop aching until sometime in January" (and that was
when the playing season ended on a day early in January).

There's nothing glamorous about aching—especially aching
for weeks and months. There is nothing headline-making about
patience—not even when we spell it in a more attractive word,
perseverance. But this is a crucial quality of faith; and the secret is
in the long view. You see something that others cannot see.

Such patience is the way we show faith in a person. It is a good
thing to applaud a musician in her senior recital. It is a better
thing to invest in the scholarship that will assure her support for
the long pull that leads to quality achievement. At no point are
the qualities of perseverance and patience more essential to faith
than in the way we relate to our fellow human beings. No
wonder, then, that we're called to run our faith-race with

perseverance. I'm sure the nineteenth-century British preacher Charles Haddon Spurgeon smiled as he spoke, but he had a point when he said, "By perseverance the snail reached the Ark."[2] Perseverance—patience—is a snail-like virtue. Its action may sometimes seem imperceptible, but it's the kind of action that is essential to the faith that triumphs.

The quality of vision that comes with faith is not simply long term or long distance; it includes clarity regarding the present. The present is so much with us that it almost always distorts our vision. We have to struggle to keep perspective. This was the problem, as the writer of Hebrews perceived it, for Moses: he had to recognize "the fleeting pleasures of sin" for what they were so he could remember that there was "greater wealth than the treasures of Egypt" (Hebrews 11:25-26). This calls for a very special kind of vision—the ability not only to see the far-off goal, but also to see the present enticements for what they are worth, namely, the present and no more! There's nothing long term about them. So much in life is withering even at the peak of its attractiveness, but it takes good vision to see that—all the more so because we live in a culture that fancies the superficial and cultivates a taste for the transient. The hit movie; the box office "attraction" (the very word has a quality of impermanence); this year's bestseller: these are the headline stuff of our world, and they change as fast as the headlines. Living in such a world distorts one's vision, gives one spiritual myopia. Faith improves our vision—not only for length, but also most assuredly for depth.

Faith may look at the scoreboard but it knows better than to be moved by it. If we're in a period of the game where God's

Kingdom seems to be far ahead, don't settle back with complacency; and if we're in a time that seems the worst of times, remember that the final score has not been posted. And never think that the game is over; and never think it will be called for rain or that action has temporarily been postponed. This game goes on without interruption.

One day our Lord will call an end to it. We declare that faith each time we say while celebrating Holy Communion, "Christ has died; Christ is risen; Christ will come again." Jesus said, however, that no one knows the day or the hour when God will call an end to the game as we know it; our business therefore is to "keep alert," to "keep awake" (Mark 13:32-37). The odds are that we will make our personal exits before the game is over. At that point we will become part of the faith-crowd that cheers on the new generation. We will know that we have done well to believe in the face of doubting, to hold steady in the times of easy compromising.

The faith that comes from God is not blind; it is extraordinary vision. It recognizes the difference between the transient and the eternal, not only between the good and the bad but also between the good and the best. It has the holy patience to hold steady, because the end is not yet—and because God's end is worth waiting and working for. A secular, today-is-all culture can't see this. Faith improves our vision beyond all human expectation.

It's because our human expectation is so small and so poor that we see faith best when we look at it from the back side.

DISCUSSION GUIDE
FOR *FAITH FROM THE BACK SIDE*
BY J. ELLSWORTH KALAS

John D. Schroeder

CHAPTER 1
FAITH FROM THE BACK SIDE

Snapshot Summary

This chapter introduces us to new ways of looking at our faith using the Letter to the Hebrews. It covers betrayal, doubt, and fear, among other topics.

Reflection / Discussion Questions

1. Share your interest in this book and what you hope to gain from your experience of reading and discussing it.

2. In your own words, explain what having faith means to you.

3. Share a faith experience from your childhood. What makes that particular experience memorable?

4. Give some more examples of how we live our lives in a world of faith.

5. What does it feel like to have your faith betrayed?

6. What can happen when faith meets fear? What does fear do to faith?

7. In what situations is your faith the strongest? When is it the weakest?

8. Discuss what we can learn about faith from the Letter to the Hebrews.

9. What gives us faith and what diminishes faith?

10. What additional thoughts or questions from this chapter would you like to explore?

Prayer

Dear God, thank you for giving us a faith that is powerful, sustaining, and life-changing. Help our faith increase as we grow in love toward you and others. Amen.

CHAPTER 2
FAITH HAS AN ATTITUDE

Snapshot Summary

This chapter explores the connection between faith and attitude using the Letter to the Hebrews. It includes the attitude that God has toward us and how we should respond.

Reflection / Discussion Questions

1. What is meant by the statement "faith has an attitude"? Give an example.

2. Share a time when you experienced faith with an attitude.

3. Reflect on / discuss the attitude that God has toward us.

4. What's the connection between faith and definitions?

5. As a Christian, what is your attitude toward life?

6. What can we learn from Jesus about faith and attitude?

7. What insights about attitude does the writer of Hebrews reveal?

8. Why can the faith-person expect to win?

9. Reflect on / discuss the types of drugging that keep us from our full potential.

10. What additional thoughts or questions from this chapter would you like to explore?

Prayer
Dear God, thank you for faith, for attitude, and for combining them into one powerful force. Show us how to live a life of faith and courage. Amen.

CHAPTER 3
FAITH HAS A HISTORY

Snapshot Summary
This chapter uses Hebrews to consider issues of faith, including the creation story, faith being older than sin, creativity, and how we are subcreators in our world.

Reflection / Discussion Questions
1. Briefly share something about the origin and history of your faith.

2. Reflect on / discuss why the creation story is hard to believe and why faith is needed.

3. How can the creation story help us improve our understanding of God?

4. Reflect on / discuss how Hebrews unfolds the story of faith at work.

5. Reflect on / discuss the reasoning why faith is older than sin.

6. Does it seem appropriate to think of God as having faith? Explain your reasoning.

7. Reflect on / discuss the role of creativity in our world and how it relates to faith.

8. How are we subcreators in our world? What impact can we have?

9. Reflect on / discuss the significance and meaning of the statement that faith is older than all of our problems.

10. What additional thoughts or questions from this chapter would you like to explore?

Prayer
Dear God, thank you for giving us a history of faith that connects us to you and our ancestors. Guide us in our role as subcreators in this world. Amen.

CHAPTER 4
FAITH SOMETIMES WALKS,
SOMETIMES FLIES

Snapshot Summary

This chapter uses the lives of Cain, Abel, and Enoch to guide us in further exploration of faith.

Reflection / Discussion Questions

1. Share a recent faith-encounter you experienced.

2. Reflect on / discuss the many faces of faith.

3. What lessons can we learn about faith from the story of Cain and Abel?

4. Reflect on / discuss the differences in faith between Cain and Abel.

5. How can Cain's lack of faith help us in our definition of faith?

6. Reflect on / discuss what it means that faith is an attitude of mind.

7. Why don't many people believe God rewards those who seek him?

8. Reflect on / discuss why we don't have to "win every game" in life. What role does faith play?

9. Reflect on / discuss Enoch and what made him so special.

10. What additional thoughts or questions from this chapter would you like to explore?

Prayer

Dear God, thank you for giving us biblical examples of faith that we can learn from and be inspired by to serve you and others in love. Amen.

CHAPTER 5
FAITH SAVES AND CONDEMNS

Snapshot Summary

This chapter uses Noah as an example of a faith that survives in tough times.

Reflection / Discussion Questions

1. Reflect on / discuss examples of times in life when it is easier to believe in God.

2. Share a time in your life when it was difficult to believe.

3. What would it have been like to live in the time of Noah?

4. How do you "out-evil" evil? Why is this necessary?

5. Reflect on / discuss some examples of the survival of goodness against evil.

6. What can we learn from the faith example of Noah?

7. Reflect on / discuss why faith needs to survive inattention as well as opposition.

8. Explain how faith can condemn as well as deliver.

9. Name some types of Noah-souls in our world today. What roles do they play?

10. What additional thoughts or questions from this chapter would you like to explore?

Prayer

Dear God, thank you for reminding us how faith saves and condemns. Help us increase our faith so it can survive against the evils of this world. Amen.

CHAPTER 6
FAITH IS A FAMILY AFFAIR

Snapshot Summary

This chapter examines the faith stories of Abraham, Isaac, and Jacob as we learn about the power of faith and family.

Reflection / Discussion Questions

1. Share how your faith is similar to or different from the faith of your parents.

2. Why is faith difficult to pass on from one generation to another?

3. How do you think Abraham must have felt about being uprooted?

4. Reflect on / discuss the faith of Sarah and what it means to have a Sarah type of faith.

5. What lessons can we learn from the life of Abraham?

6. How do you think Abraham conveyed his faith to Isaac?

7. Reflect on / discuss the lessons of faith found in the story of God asking Abraham to use Isaac as an offering.

8. Reflect on / discuss why the names *Abraham, Jacob,* and *Isaac* might be called the rhythm of faith.

9. How did Jacob and Isaac follow in the footsteps of faith of Abraham?

10. What additional thoughts or questions from this chapter would you like to explore?

Prayer

Dear God, thank you for faith that can be passed along and influenced by family members. Help us keep each other strong in faith. Amen.

CHAPTER 7
FAITH TAKES A TEST

Snapshot Summary

Further exploring the story of Abraham and Isaac, this chapter looks at situations in life that test our faith.

Reflection / Discussion Questions

1. Share a time when your faith was tested.
2. Reflect on / discuss situations in life that test our faith.
3. What qualities does it take to pass a test of faith?
4. Why do some people fail a test of faith?
5. When you read the story of Abraham and Isaac, what thoughts come to mind?
6. Why do you think Abraham was obedient to God's request?
7. What does this story tell us about God?
8. Reflect on / discuss the possible thoughts, feelings, and questions of Isaac during this journey.
9. Why do you think this story is included in the Bible? What impact does it have?
10. What additional thoughts or questions from this chapter would you like to explore?

Prayer

Dear God, thank you for giving us the ability to pass the tests of life using our faith in you. Amen.

CHAPTER 8
FAITH CAN BE COMMUNICATED

Snapshot Summary

This chapter uses the life stories of Joseph, Rahab, and others to explore the seeds of faith and how faith is communicated among people.

Reflection / Discussion Questions

1. Share a time when you witnessed faith in action, communicated by word or deed.

2. List some of the many ways faith can be communicated.

3. Reflect on / discuss what helps and hinders the process of sharing faith with others.

4. Why does the author call this the generation of the faithful? Do you agree?

5. Reflect on / discuss why faith is a hardy gift.

6. How did Joseph plant the seed of faith and encourage the communication of faith?

7. Reflect on / discuss the impact of Rahab's faith and actions.

8. How does the Holy Spirit help us in communicating faith?

9. List some of the basics of how to and how not to communicate faith to others.

10. What additional thoughts or questions from this chapter would you like to explore?

Prayer

Dear God, thank you for a faith that deserves to and needs to be shared with others. Help us share Jesus. Amen.

CHAPTER 9
FAITH HAS THE LONG VIEW

Snapshot Summary

This chapter examines faith that was there before us and will be around long after we are gone. Moses is used as an example of a person with a long view of faith.

Reflection / Discussion Questions

1. Describe some times when impatience surrounds us.

2. Reflect on / discuss the benefits of faith having a long view.

3. How is faith like a work of art? Describe the similarities.

4. Why is the life of Moses a good example of the long view of faith?

5. What lessons about faith can we learn from the life of Moses?

6. How much are we products of our ancestry, and how much are we products of our environment?

7. When and where do you think Moses began to learn that faith has a long view?

8. Reflect on / discuss where Moses got his faith. Name some of the sources.

9. Why did Moses turn his back on the fleeting pleasures of Egypt?

10. What additional thoughts or questions from this chapter would you like to explore?

Prayer

Dear God, thank you for a faith that is long and lasting. Guide us as we share our faith with those who need Jesus. Amen.

CHAPTER 10
FAITH'S HEROES ARE A MIXED LOT

Snapshot Summary

This chapter looks at Old Testament heroes of all kinds, with their strengths, weaknesses, and faith.

Reflection / Discussion Questions

1. Reflect on / discuss the qualifications of being a faith hero today or in biblical times.

2. Why are faith heroes a mixed lot?

3. Reflect on / discuss why Rahab is a hero.

4. What impresses you about Gideon as a faith hero?

5. Why does Barak belong to the list of heroes? Why does his co-leader Deborah?

6. Reflect on / discuss the faith of Samson and why he is also a hero.

7. How did Jephthah serve God? Why does he fit the hero category?

8. What did David teach us about having faith?

9. List some ways we can be faith heroes by word or deed.

10. What additional thoughts or questions from this chapter would you like to explore?

Prayer

Dear God, thank you for faith heroes who made a difference and who continue to inspire us. Amen.

CHAPTER 11
FAITH MAKES US TOUGH

Snapshot Summary

This chapter explores more insights about faith from Hebrews and looks at the example of the three men who faced the furnace of fire.

Reflection / Discussion Questions

1. Explain what a tough faith means to you.

2. Share how faith has made you tough.

3. When did you first learn that *faith* is a tough word?

4. Reflect on / discuss the faith of the three young men who faced the furnace because of their faith.

5. What new insights does the writer of Hebrews offer about faith and toughness?

6. Reflect on / discuss the many ways faith shows itself, often with unexpected outcomes.

7. How should the effectiveness of faith be measured?

8. List some of the benefits of tough faith.

9. Explain what is meant by the statement "Faith has nothing to do with the scoreboard."

10. What additional thoughts or questions from this chapter would you like to explore?

Prayer

Dear God, thank you for a faith that makes us tough and able to withstand all that comes our way. Amen.

CHAPTER 12
FAITH SEES WHAT OTHERS CANNOT

Snapshot Summary

This final chapter looks at our faith vision, how our eyes are opened, and why patience and perseverance are needed for faith to thrive.

Reflection / Discussion Questions

1. Share a time when faith opened your eyes and helped you see more clearly.

2. Reflect on / discuss what the writer of Hebrews says in Hebrews 11:13-16.

3. How do you measure faith?

4. How and why does faith improve our vision?

5. List some of the ways the world distorts our faith vision.

6. Reflect on / discuss how and why patience and perseverance are essential qualities of faith.

7. How are the eyes of faith opened? Share some tips on how to achieve this.

8. Reflect on / discuss why we see faith best when we see it from the back side.

9. What additional thoughts or questions from this chapter would you like to explore?

10. How has this book and your reflections or discussions about it helped you learn more about faith?

Prayer

Dear God, thank you for this small-group experience, and for allowing us to learn about and grow in faith. Amen.

Notes

1. Faith from the Back Side

1. William Cowper, "God Moves in a Mysterious Way," in *The Book of Hymns* (Nashville: The Methodist Publishing House, 1964, 1966), 215.

2. Quoted in Margaret Pepper, *The Harper Religious & Inspirational Quotation Companion* (New York: Harper & Row, 1989), 156.

2. Faith Has an Attitude

1. Martin Luther, "A Mighty Fortress Is Our God," in *The United Methodist Hymnal* (Nashville: The United Methodist Publishing House, 1989), 110.

2. John Richard Green, *A Short History of the English People* (1874), chap. 7.

3. *The Interpreter's Bible*, vol. 10 (Nashville: Abingdon Press, 1953), 508.

3. Faith Has a History

1. Robert Alter, *The Five Books of Moses* (New York: W. W. Norton, 2004), 17.

2. Ursula Goodenough, *The Sacred Depths of Nature* (New York: Oxford University Press, 1998), 4–5.

3. Humphrey Carpenter, *The Inklings* (Boston: Houghton Mifflin, 1978), 138.

4. Faith Sometimes Walks, Sometimes Flies

1. Robert Alter, *The Five Books of Moses* (New York: W. W. Norton, 2004), 29.

2. Tertullian, A.D. c. 160–c. 225: "As often as we are mown down by you, the more we grow in numbers; the blood of Christians is the seed."

3. C. S. Lewis, *Surprised by Joy* (New York: Harcourt, Brace, 1955), 228, 229.

5. Faith Saves and Condemns

1. William Barclay, *The Letter to the Hebrews* (Philadelphia: Westminster Press, 1957), 160.

7. Faith Takes a Test

1. Harvey Cushing, *The Life of Sir William Osler*, vol. 2 (Oxford: Oxford at the Clarendon Press, 1925), chap. 30.

8. Faith Can Be Communicated

1. Cuthbert Bardsley and William Purcell, *Him We Declare* (Waco, Texas: Word Books, 1968), 43.

11. Faith Makes Us Tough

1. Marilyn Chandler McEntyre, *Caring for Words in a Culture of Lies* (Grand Rapids: William B. Eerdmans, 2009), 29.

12. Faith Sees What Others Cannot

1. Quoted in *Bartlett's Familiar Quotations*, 17th ed., ed. Justin Kaplan (New York: Little, Brown, 2002), 508.

2. Quoted in Margaret Pepper, *The Harper Religious & Inspirational Quotation Companion* (New York: Harper & Row, 1989), 316.